LEADERSHIP
and the
Art of Change

To Professor Lehman Benson III, friend and colleague,
without whom this book would never have come to be.

LEADERSHIP
and the
Art of Change

A Practical Guide to Organizational Transformation

Lee Roy Beach

University of Arizona

SAGE Publications
Thousand Oaks ▪ London ▪ New Delhi

For information:

 Sage Publications, Inc.
2455 Teller Road
Thousand Oaks, California 91320
E-mail: order@sagepub.com

Sage Publications Ltd.
1 Oliver's Yard
55 City Road
London EC1Y 1SP
United Kingdom

Sage Publications India Pvt. Ltd.
B-42, Panchsheel Enclave
Post Box 4109
New Delhi 110 017 India

Library of Congress Cataloging-in-Publication Data

Beach, Lee Roy.
Leadership and the art of change / Lee Roy Beach.
   p. cm.
Includes bibliographical references and index.
ISBN 978-1-4129-1381-2 (cloth) — ISBN 978-1-4129-1382-9 (pbk.)
   1. Leadership. 2. Organizational change. I. Title.
HD57.7.B43 2006
658.4′092—dc22

                           2005003050

This book is printed on acid-free paper.

10   11   12   13 8 7 6 5 4 3

Acquisitions Editor:	Al Bruckner
Editorial Assistant:	MaryAnn Vail
Production Editor:	Diane S. Foster
Copy Editor:	Robert Holm
Typesetter:	C&M Digitals (P) Ltd.
Proofreader:	Jamie Robinson
Indexer:	Molly Hall
Cover Designer:	Michelle Kenny

Contents

Acknowledgments

Portions of this book are adapted from L. R. Beach (1993), *Making the Right Decision: Organizational Culture, Vision and Planning*, Englewood Cliffs, N.J., (Prentice Hall), by permission of the author and copyright holder. Appendix A is adapted from L. R. Beach and L. R. Burns (1995), "The Service Quality Improvement Strategy: Identifying Priorities for Change," *International Journal of Service Industry Management*, 6, pp. 5–15; and L. R. Burns and L. R. Beach (1994), "The Quality Improvement Strategy," *Health Care Management Review, 19*, pp. 21–31, by permission of the authors and copyright holders.

The saga of the Steller Art Frame Company, recounted throughout this book, is based on a real company. However, as the details were altered for illustrative purposes, Steller became so thoroughly fictionalized that it bears no resemblance to any specific company with which I am familiar.

Preface

*L*eadership and the Art of Change is for students and practitioners who want a practical framework for successfully leading organizational change. Leadership is the art of producing appropriate changes in an organization's external environment, its functions and structure, its culture, and its practices in pursuit of survival and prosperity. The framework for the book is provided by a list of six prime responsibilities that leaders must meet in order to bring about successful change. They must work with others within the organization (1) to understand the organization's internal and external environments, (2) to understand the organization's culture, (3) to create a vision of a desirable future and obtain buy-in, (4) to design a plan that moves the organization toward the envisioned future, (5) to integrate the various units in implementation of the plan and to monitor progress, and (6) to institutionalize achieved changes and make continuous change an integral part of the organization's culture.

To aid in mastery of the material, the summary of each chapter is left as an exercise for the reader, using an outline of the chapter as a guide. To the same end, each chapter is followed by a new segment of an ongoing exercise that helps the reader form his or her own understanding of the issues. This is followed by a list of sources and materials for further study. At the end of the book, three appendixes provide illustrative methods for assessing customer needs (Appendix A), assessing the organization's culture (Appendix B), and making complex decisions (Appendix C).

I would like to thank the countless executives who have educated me about the practical aspects of leadership and who have shared with me their knowledge about promoting organizational change. Some of these people have been clients with whom I worked as the change process unfolded. Others have been participants in executive education courses from whom I learned far more than they learned from me. I hope that this book repays in some measure their generosity in sharing their experiences with me.

—Lee Roy Beach
Tucson, Arizona

Introduction

Leadership: Championing Change

Looking around his office at all the boxes waiting for the moving crew, Wayne felt angry . . . and his stomach ached. He wished he knew which box contained his stomach pills.

Oddly enough, at the lowest point in his career his prospects never looked better. He was going to a new job at a higher-profile company, in a bigger city, and at higher pay. Still, he knew he wasn't leaving in triumph: His record looked better on paper than it actually was. He had brought in some high-profile customers, invested in some cutting-edge technology, and made a very visible (if short-lived) partnership with a big name manufacturer, but in fact he had failed.

This had been his big opportunity to test his leadership abilities. Before he came, the company had been in a slow decline. The board of directors wanted to reverse this, prepare for changes in the industry, and achieve more visibility. They wanted someone to shake things up, infuse a sense of direction, build bridges, and generally prepare the company for the future.

Wayne had honestly thought he was the right person. He had held jobs at almost every level, moving from one company to another in his upward climb. In his last job, he had spent 3 years as the right-hand man to the CEO, which he felt gave him the experience he needed to take the top spot somewhere. When an executive search agency approached him about this job, he jumped at it. He flew in for an interview, which went well, if only because of his obvious enthusiasm. A few days later he received word that he had been selected.

He arrived to a warm reception. It turned out that the previous CEO had not been well liked. Wayne, and his enthusiasm, seemed like a breath of fresh air. It was clear that people were hungry for energetic, imaginative leadership, and that was what he intended to supply.

His first 2 weeks on the job were spent in his office, usually alone, planning the changes he intended to make in the company. He thought of himself as a "hired gun"—like in a Western movie—the solitary figure that arrives in a cloud of dust, fights the bad guys, saves the town, is cheered by the townsfolk, and then rides off into the sunset. In this scenario, he didn't have to know a lot about the particular company he was saving. The important thing was to know how to save it. And, he was sure he knew how.

He began by comparing this company with the others at which he had worked and, where it differed, thinking of ways he could make it more like the others. Out of this evolved a list of goals and then a set of initiatives that he thought would achieve those goals, which he termed "The Plan."

Things started to go wrong when he rolled out The Plan at a meeting with his department managers. When the meeting opened, everyone was friendly and the mood was upbeat. He began by presenting his list of goals for the company. Without pause, he described the set of initiatives that he had designed to move the company toward the goals. He tried to be analytic and logical, and he thought he might even have been a little eloquent. But when he asked for questions, there was only silence.

Finally, a hand went up near the back of the room. The sales manager cleared her throat and said, in a voice so low that Wayne had to strain to hear, that she was sorry but she didn't understand where the goals came from and she couldn't see any common thread connecting them. Moreover, although she may have misunderstood, it seemed like some of them were so ill-defined that it wasn't clear how to achieve them: "Become an industry leader," for example. It also seemed to her that some of the initiatives were at cross-purposes with each other. And, wouldn't undertaking all of the initiatives at once be extremely disruptive and enormously expensive? She finished by saying, apologetically, that perhaps her mind had wandered when Wayne had outlined the "big picture" that made sense of everything and would he please go over it again?

"Well, Ms. Smarty Pants," Wayne thought angrily to himself, "there isn't a 'big picture' to go over again because there wasn't one in the first place." Not bothering to hide his displeasure, he ignored her questions and launched into a lecture about his leadership philosophy. Sure, somewhere he had read that leaders ought to have a big picture, a guiding vision, but he had never been clear about what that meant and suspected it was merely touchy-feely jargon. His leadership didn't need a big picture because it had three simple themes: opportunism, problem solving, and delegation.

Opportunism meant that as the leader, it was his responsibility to spot opportunities for the company and to pursue them. *Problem solving* meant that it was his responsibility to identify problems with the company and to formulate solutions to them. *Delegation* meant that it was his managers' responsibility to see that employees carried out his plans for pursuing the opportunities and solving the problems. By the time he finished his lecture, the room had become even quieter.

Three days later, a written document containing his goals and initiatives, labeled "The Plan" in big black letters, was distributed to all managers. It was accompanied by a request that they identify those parts for which their units would take the lead and that they submit a written proposal describing what this entailed. The proposal was due by the end of the week, no exceptions or extensions!

Two months later, all the proposals had finally trickled in and were given to a secretary to collate. The resulting compendium of vague promises was then edited by Wayne to reflect his goals and declared to be "The Final Plan." Copies were sent to the board members and all company employees, some of whom read it.

After this rough beginning, Wayne was convinced that things could only get better. They didn't. Three managers, including Ms. Smarty Pants, quit and had to be replaced with less-experienced people. Turnover also increased on the shop floor as some of his most experienced workers sought jobs elsewhere. Even worse, meetings to discuss progress with his managers began with their excuses and ended with his ill-tempered monologues.

Wayne hadn't realized how much opposition there was to The Final Plan until the local newspaper ran an article about the company. He was shocked to see employees saying that the very integrity of the company was at stake, that the things they were being asked to do flew in the face of everything the company had always stood for, that they had worked hard for years only to be ordered to undermine all that they had helped build. What were these people talking about? They seemed to believe that what he was trying to do was threatening the company instead of making things better. Clearly, his managers would have to work harder to counteract this stuff.

It soon became evident that even those few managers who were on his side were having trouble rallying support. Everywhere he looked he saw resistance to even the slightest change. At first he put this down to simple distrust of anything new, confident that a few successes would win hearts and minds and bring more people on board. But even successes didn't bring buy-in. Not only were employees resistant, they seemed confused. It was as though they didn't know why they were doing what they were asked to do, for which he blamed the managers.

After months of glacial progress, Wayne decided that it was time to dazzle everyone with some opportunism. He had heard that two major customers were concerned about rising costs, so he offered them discounts for purchasing exclusively from his company. There was little profit in this for the company, but everyone sat up and took notice, and he expected his boldness would change some bad attitudes. It didn't.

Next, he bought exclusive rights to a new technology that he was convinced would revolutionize the industry. He severely cut budgets throughout the company to bring this off, only to see the technology sit unused most of the time. It was so fast that it outran everything else and had to be shut down periodically so everything else could catch up. Again, nobody was impressed.

Then he swung a deal to partner with a very high-profile company to comarket a product with both their names on it. The partnership ran at a slight loss, but the visibility it provided seemed to him to be invaluable. After about 6 months, the other company pulled out, citing both the loss and the fact that they didn't gain much by the association with his company. This time everyone noticed, but they clearly didn't like what they saw.

Finally, he let it be known that he had been approached about merging with a competitor. This never got far because everybody around him seemed to come unhinged. The board members were furious that he had leaked the news before they had even discussed it. His managers were furious because they saw their jobs in jeopardy. The rank-and-file employees were furious because they felt they were being sold out. Even his secretary stopped being nice to him. He began to see the handwriting on the wall.

It didn't take him long to make inquiries about another job. Lots of places needed experienced executives, and his career looked great on paper. True, he had been in his present job only a short time, but it was easy to argue that the company was too hidebound to make the changes demanded by an innovative leader. Clearly, any bright young man on the rise shouldn't waste time on a company that has a death wish; he should go where his talents could be appreciated.

But in his heart Wayne knew he had failed. What made it rough was that he realized that if even he could start all over, he wouldn't know what to do differently. His leadership philosophy had let him down, and he didn't know what to do about it. Perhaps the answer had something to do with the big picture, but he didn't have a clue what it could be.

Poor Wayne. With the best of intentions and an abundance of enthusiasm, he did just what he thought leaders are supposed to do: He took command. He identified what he thought were problems and came up with what he thought were solutions. He was decisive. He was forceful. He honestly tried to guide the company toward a brighter future. And all he got for his trouble was resistance, rebellion, and people quitting. It hardly seems fair.

Role Playing, Charisma, and Authentic Leadership

Like so many people who find themselves in positions of leadership, it appears that Poor Wayne simply failed to understand the difference between playing the role of a leader and actually being a leader. Because leaders promote change, he didn't bother to learn much about the company because he was going to change everything anyway. Because leaders are decisive, he single-handedly identified problems, came up with solutions, and then told the managers what he had decided to do. Because leaders are firm, he used anger to intimidate his managers and squelch further opposition without weighing the merits of their arguments. Small wonder he failed; simply posing as a leader does not work because it focuses on the surface features of leadership and is blind to the underlying art of leading an organization toward meaningful change.

Actually, "Poor Wayne" is a composite of people we all have known, each of whom failed to understand the organization they were supposed to lead, each of whom sought a formula for identifying and solving problems without a larger view of what caused the problems or how the solutions would improve things, and each of whom lacked a framework to help them think constructively about change and how to go about it. Sure, they boned up on production, finance, marketing, and the organization chart. But they fail to learn about the environment in which the organization operated or about the heart of the organization: what it is now, what its members believe it is striving to become, and how that striving can be channeled in directions that ultimately will help it prosper in its environment. Indeed, they assume that the only way to lead is to be tough, make massive changes, and force recalcitrant subordinates to do things a new way. They equate their own doubt with weakness and others' doubt with treachery. They regard even reasonable questions as signs of opposition and obstruction. And, of course, they alienate everyone who could help them do their jobs successfully. True, some of them catch on fast enough to save themselves. But others simply fail and move on.

Role-playing is far more difficult than authentic leadership because the player does not know what he or she is trying to accomplish, except to win. Eventually, this shallowness will be detected by others, making them distrustful and resistant. Role-playing gets even more difficult if the new leader believes that he or she has to be charismatic as well. Charisma is the ability to galvanize the emotions and actions of others and, in doing so, lead them in directions that they would not otherwise have gone. There are schools that can teach you to be charming and likable, but there are no schools that can teach you to be charismatic: You either have charisma or not. Acting like you do won't work.

Even leaders who possess charisma often fail. Charisma does not wear well as an everyday thing: It is most suitable in crises, which are, by definition, exceptions to the usual run of events. In fact, charisma can actually interfere with day-to-day functioning of an organization and, as a result, decrease its performance. This is because charisma, in contrast to mere charm, serves to mobilize people to surmount difficulties; but an organization that is constantly mobilized, or is mobilized disproportionately to its problems, quickly burns out. People get tired. Moreover, they are too busy to concentrate on the mundane, day-to-day tasks that keep the enterprise running.

So, what about authentic leaders, those who avoid role-playing and seek to behave with substance and good sense? Well, they clearly do not attempt to simply mimic the behavior of charismatic leaders. Nor do they memorize a list of rules about what to do in this or that situation. Nor do they seize on the latest quick fix from the best seller list or seminar circuit. Instead, they act like what they are: intelligent people who are trying to do a good job while being decent, reasonable, and responsible.

Authentic leaders understand that the task for every organization is to survive and prosper, where prospering means successful pursuit of its goals. They understand that the leader's fundamental job is to help the organization change in light of changes in its environment so that it can accomplish its task of surviving and prospering.

Authentic leaders place the interests of their organizations above their own. They recognize that they are there to serve their organizations, to further their organizations' ambitions rather than their own. They know that that their personal success will follow naturally from their organization's success, an insight that frees them to focus on promoting its success rather than on self-promotion.

Authentic leaders know that crises will occur and that they will have to help people rise to the occasion. But, they also know that crises will pass, and it is what they do over the long haul that makes the most difference. They know that success depends on their subordinates, with whom they must deal honestly and respectfully. They know that short of a religious conversion, a traumatic experience, or brain damage, an adult's personality is unlikely to change. So what they are now is pretty much what they will be in the future, and this is true of those around them as well. They know that good leaders build on their own and others' strengths and try to neutralize or negate their own and others' weaknesses. In short, they know that leadership largely consists of knowing their organizations and their coworkers, knowing their own jobs, being responsible, and making the most of what they have.

Finally, authentic leaders know that leadership is about change that will move the organization toward a better future. They know that to promote change, they must learn the art of change, which consists of meeting six prime responsibilities.

Leaders' Six Prime Responsibilities

1. *Assessment:* Leaders must work with others in the organization to assess the organization's external and internal environments and specify needed changes in each.

2. *Culture:* Leaders must work with others in the organization to understand the organization's culture: the core beliefs and values that are shared by the organization's members, that guide their actions in its behalf and define their expectations about the actions of those around them. If the culture impedes progress, they must work with others to change the culture appropriately.

3. *Vision:* Leaders must work with others in the organization to create a vision, a reasonable story about the organization's future in light of the

constraints imposed by its environment and culture, and to articulate the goal agenda that follows from that vision. Then they must promote acceptance of the vision throughout the organization.

4. *Plans:* Leaders must work with others in the organization to design a plan for moving the organization toward the envisioned future and to promote understanding throughout the organization of how that plan will address the goal agenda in pursuit of the vision.

5. *Implementation:* Leaders must work with others to maintain momentum during plan implementation and to monitor progress in order to discover and correct weaknesses in the plan.

6. *Follow-Through:* Leaders must work with others to institutionalize achieved changes and to help members accept ongoing change as a normal aspect of the organization and its activities.

Each of the six chapters in this book explores one of the six prime responsibilities. For ease of exposition, I will talk throughout the book as though you, the reader, are the chief executive of a medium-to-large organization that needs to undergo substantial change. Moreover, I usually will talk as though your organization is a for-profit business. Talking this way, however, does not mean that the six prime responsibilities apply only to businesses. On the contrary, they apply to all types of organizations, but they must be intelligently adapted to fit the specific characteristics of other kinds of organizations. Nor does it mean that leadership is limited to the chief executive; any member of the organization who is in the position to undertake the six prime responsibilities can be a leader, although the details of the responsibilities must be adapted to the circumstances. In the Conclusion, I will discuss some of these adaptations and expand our analysis of change to nonprofit and governmental organizations and to other levels of management.

Poor Wayne, Again

Before we move on, consider Poor Wayne again. Suppose that he had taken time to learn about the company he had come to lead. Suppose he had found that it had a tradition of participative decision making, that people there believed that they had something to contribute, and that they expected management to take advantage of that contribution. Suppose that they were used to talking directly with the company officers and that they were used to their opinions being respected. Suppose that they thought of the company as a professional organization in which orders were not simply given and obeyed in a mechanical way. Suppose that, although they valued survival of the company and preservation of their jobs, they did not believe that the slavish imitation of solutions that worked at other companies would necessarily work at theirs.

Suppose that Wayne had learned that his managers already knew what was wrong with the company. Suppose he had understood that the employees were bright enough and talented enough to adapt their activities to a new vision, if it addressed practical problems and offered a sufficiently inspiring big picture. Suppose he had listened instead of talking.

If Wayne had bothered to learn all of this before he began, his decisions probably would have been different. Instead of trying to make this company look like the company he used to work in, he could have worked with his managers and the employees to build the unique vision this company needed to succeed in its unique environment. They could have built a vision that respected their beliefs and values—but that addressed the particular problems the environment presented—and provided a plan that gave direction and coherence to any change initiative.

Poor Wayne is more to be pitied than scorned. He probably did not realize that to promote organizational change, one must know where the organization is to start with, where the changes are designed to take it, and what the various constraints are on what it can do. He may never have known that organizations have cultures, and if he did, he may have thought it was only an interesting oddity. He never understood what a vision is (the big picture), so by default, he sought to lead this company toward some ideal composite of the desirable features of other companies he had worked for. He knew plans are good, but because his faulty vision failed to define how his company should adapt to its business environment, the initiatives that composed his plan may or may not have addressed issues central to the company's survival and future prosperity.

Lacking such understanding, Wayne attributed his failure to employee rebellion and ingratitude. It didn't occur to him that his good intentions weren't enough. In short, despite his job experience and his confidence in his readiness for leadership responsibility, Poor Wayne did not know very much.

Summary

To aid in mastery of the foregoing material, summarize it for yourself it by filling in this topic outline.

Leadership: Championing Change

I. Poor Wayne (vignette)

II. Role playing, charisma, and authentic leadership

III. Leaders' six prime responsibilities
   A. Assessment
   B. Culture
   C. Vision
   D. Plans
   E. Implementation
   F. Institutionalization

IV. Poor Wayne, again

One

Assessment: Specifying Change

Prime Responsibility #1: Leaders must work with others in the organization to assess the organization's external and internal environments and specify needed changes in each.

Leadership is about change but not arbitrary change. Change can exact a huge price. Aside from resources tied up implementing functional and structural changes—in new systems, equipment, training, or personnel—there is an enormous cost in extra effort and disruption of routines. If nothing else, the organization is almost always less efficient while it undergoes change. Unless it has sufficient excess capacity to compensate, this inefficiency can adversely affect production of goods or services with a resulting loss of customers and compromised relations with suppliers and other stakeholders. Moreover, change is hard on the members of organizations; emotions run high, people work long hours, things seldom go strictly according to plan. Change is not to be undertaken lightly, certainly not for any but the most compelling reasons.

Although change for its own sake clearly is foolish, it is equally clear that an organization can be in trouble if it does not change in response to the dynamics of its internal and external environments. Therefore, it is a prime responsibility of a leader to work with others in the organization to assess the organization's external and internal environments, where *assess* means acquiring and interpreting information about the environments. This usually consists of information about the current status of the external and internal environments, forecasts of future status of the environments, and indications of the present and future intentions and desires of stakeholders (customers or potential customers, suppliers, shareholders, employees, the community, and to some extent, competitors). The goal is to create a picture of how the organization, with its unique internal environment, functions within its unique external environment. This in turn permits identification of existing and potential opportunities and threats and dictates the changes, external and internal to the organization, that must be made in order to address them.

Assessing the External Environment

Assessment of the external environment, often called environmental scanning, is the process of acquiring information about the presence and nature of external demands and constraints on the organization's actions. One might think of an organization as involved in a game with its competitors. The playing field for this game is the organization's external environment, defined by the ever changing rules imposed by the forces at work within that environment (e.g., industry practices; the local, national, and world economy; government regulations; resource availability; and social trends and customer preferences). Assessment of this environment is aimed at understanding the structure of the playing field and the rules of the game, its existing and potential opportunities and threats. Within the bounds of this understanding, the strategies used by the organization in its attempt to win (or at least stay in the game) depend on its internal environment: its structure and how it operates, the nature of its culture, its vision for its future, and its ability to focus its efforts on achievement of its vision. The leader's job is to make the organization a viable participant in this game by fostering an understanding of its external and internal environments and by promoting changes in both of them that enhance its ability react to or anticipate opportunities and threats, with the goal of surviving and prospering.

Environmental assessment is done at every level of the organization. On the "shop floor" (in whatever way that is defined for a particular organization), supervisors strive to be informed about what is going on and what part they and their subordinates play in the overall endeavor. At the next levels, managers strive to be informed, about both events within the organization and, to some degree, events external to the organization. At the highest levels, the organization's leaders strive to be informed as broadly as possible about events internal to the organization as well as events in the external environment.

Every successful leader I know is almost as well informed about the world in general as he or she is about his or her own organization. Most of these people are well educated, well traveled, and well connected. They know what is going on in the world and have a pretty good idea about how it will affect their organizations now and in the future. Their skill as leaders turns heavily on their ability to convince the members of their organizations to follow them on paths that are based on this fund of knowledge. Their workdays typically revolve around two activities: learning more about the organization's external and internal environments and translating what they learn into a steadily evolving vision, a coherent, reasonable story about the future that the members of their organizations can understand and willingly pursue.

Buying Information

Information about the external environment often is harder to obtain than information about the internal environment. Moreover, although all information is expensive, external information frequently is very expensive, so users must decide what they want and how much they are willing to invest in obtaining it. It is convenient to think of four levels of investment in information procurement and the sources typically linked with each. A low level of investment buys information from such sources as one's own knowledge and hunches, others' knowledge and hunches, or easily obtained data such as changes in monthly sales of one's products, number of customer complaints, or a competitor's exit from or entry into one's markets. Payment for this information usually is in the form of buying lunch in exchange for knowledge, hunches, opinions or advice, asking employees to do a little more work to tabulate demand or complaint data, or watching the newspapers for competitors' advertisements or articles about them in the business pages.

A medium-low level of investment buys all of the above plus generally available information from industry or government sources. Some industry sources are trade magazines, trade association information services, and the Internet, either free or from subscription services that compile industry- and product-specific data, informed analysis, and forecasts. Some government sources are the Census Bureau (www.census.gov), the Department of Commerce (www.commerce.gov), and the Small Business Administration (www.sba.gov). Payment is in the form of acquiring computer literacy and, in some cases, a subscription fee. Sometimes the problem is that there is so much available, of every possible description and reliability, it's difficult to find the specific information you need, and it's worse when you aren't really sure what you need. You can obtain more targeted information, cheaply, from your public library or local college or university libraries. Seek out the business librarian, a vastly underappreciated resource, who can help you find information in the library's collection, suggest sources you never dreamed existed, and direct you to relevant Web sites.

A medium-high level of investment buys even more information, this time from empirical tests. Here your product (a term that includes both goods and services) is introduced to a potential new market, or a new or retooled product is introduced to an existing market. Often this is done in a few representative sites just to test customer acceptance. If acceptance is there, the experiment is expanded; if not, the product is dropped. Payment is in the form of the cost of the experiment, such as an advertising campaign and distribution expenses. A manufacturer of ketchup, for example, might be considering adding a chili flavored variety to its product line and wants to know if people will buy it. Test markets could be set up in Albuquerque, Milwaukee, Philadelphia, and Sacramento, with an advertising blitz in each city. If everybody loves the new flavor, the manufacturer can consider marketing the new product across the country. If it is liked only in Albuquerque, the manufacturer might consider distributing the new product only in the Southwest. If it turns out that nobody likes the new flavor, the manufacturer can quietly drop the whole idea and be glad that an expensive and ill-fated product launch was avoided.

A high level of investment buys consultants or an in-house research group that can monitor all the other lower-cost sources of information, can perform surveys and other forms of market research, and can tap expert opinion about national and world trends and their implications for opportunities and threats for the organization.

Organizations do not devote the same amount of effort and money to assessment of every sector of their external environments. Common sense dictates that investment be heavier in sectors of particular interest to the organization and in sectors about which there is greater uncertainty and volatility. A pharmaceutical company, for example, might invest heavily in information about public opinion about the retail cost of drugs and about the views of legislators about how to reduce such costs because both public opinion and legislators' views are volatile. The same organization might invest less heavily in information about, say, regional real estate prices or labor costs in Third World nations because, at the moment, neither has a direct impact on their business interests.

In fact, most businesses spend their external assessment budgets rather narrowly, primarily on market research to acquire information about their customers' needs in relation to the business's products. Appendix A contains an example of a market research tool that a colleague and I developed for a large hospital that faced falling revenues due to an increase in competition from other regional hospitals. Administrators wanted to know which of the many services the hospital provided were regarded by its customers (which, surprisingly, are physicians rather than patients) as falling short of, equaling, or exceeding their needs. The information allowed the hospital to optimize its expenditures by cutting back on over-provided services, leaving acceptable services as they were, and expanding underprovided services to better meet customer needs. This resulted in increased physician willingness to send patients to the hospital.

This kind of research is expensive because it requires a trained survey staff that can ensure that the sample of customers is representative so the results will be valid. Moreover, they must analyze the data and interpret the results for top managers, who usually lack research skills. Most organizations employ market research organizations or college/university consultants to conduct their more complicated information procurement.

A relatively new profession has developed as librarians and information specialists have opened shop to provide secondary research for businesses and other organizations. These people, informally, call themselves "information brokers," and they search out data that are available on the Internet and in other archival sources. The information they provide is called secondary because it is amassed by other people, like survey companies, government agencies, or trade organizations. But unlike most of us, information brokers know where to look for specific answers to their clients' specific questions, and they have access to databases that most of us do not. They work on a client-by-client basis for negotiated fees.

Descriptions of services offered by information brokers, as well as contact information that will help in selecting a broker, can be found on the Association of Independent Information Professionals (AIIP) Web site (www.aiip.org). Among the diverse services offered are summaries of information about competitors or statistics about product demand, government and public policy documents, data mining or warehousing, patent searches, lists of upcoming trade shows, and copies of papers presented at scientific meetings. AIIP's contact information allows you to pick a broker that specializes in the kind(s) of work you need done. For example, one company on the AIIP contact list, Bancroft Information Services (www .bancroftinfo.com), offers to provide client and customer leads for specific services and products; the history, personnel, news stories, and other information about competitors; fact checking; industry trends and statistics; and consulting services related to effective design of your own in-house information management and research systems. To better explain its services, Bancroft's site provides descriptions of some of its projects. For example, "A publisher was planning to launch a very specific health care–related publication to a small segment of the health care market. Research was performed to determine the current market for such a niche periodical, including information on current competing products and buying habits of the potential audience."

Walk Around

Most of the assessment methods described above involve secondary sources or special research tools. But we must not overlook the importance of face-to-face discussions about the external environment with people both inside the organization and outside. Longtime employees probably know a great deal about your customers and suppliers, about recent market trends and innovations that have yet to emerge. Retired employees, particularly those who have been in leadership positions, can fill you in on the history of the organization: how it came to be what it is and how it has dealt with previous opportunities and threats. Industry consultants can help you understand the environment and provide informed forecasts of future developments. Industry colleagues like to talk shop, and conventions and industry meetings provide opportunities to learn from them.

Further afield, state and local leaders can provide information about current issues that face organizations such as yours, as well as predictions about what the future will bring. Local legislation often has a greater than anticipated impact on organizations, even those whose customers are elsewhere (tax policy, for example).

Finally, get to know the faculty at the nearest college or university. If your organization is a business, the business faculty is a source of thoughtful analysis and information about new management techniques. If your organization isn't a business, you should get to know faculty in fields related to your organization's activities, but knowing the business faculty is still a good idea. Faculty members often are willing to help with specific problems, either by consulting or by having their classes undertake projects that address the problems. Volunteer to be on the advisory board for the program(s) of interest; you can use your expertise to help them, and they'll use theirs to help you. Don't overlook the economics department. Every organization should have access to an economist, if only to decode the analyses you come across in newspapers and magazines.

Where to Look

So much is available about an organization's external environment that tools are helpful in structuring the search for relevant information and guiding its assessment. One such tool is the search matrix (Fig. 1.1). The parts of the search matrix that are relevant will differ from one organization to another, but it is easy to customize the matrix to any particular organization.

The matrix has two dimensions: sectors and participants.

Sectors. Most organizations' external environments can be divided into five sectors, each of which can affect them and over which they have only limited control:

1. *The economy* at the local, national, and global levels affects the demand for products, the demand for shares, the availability of funds, and the size of the labor pool.

2. *Government* at the local, national, and global levels affects the ease of carrying out an organization's mission through regulation, taxation, and the provision of trained workforce through education and training programs.

3. *Society* at the local, national, and global levels affects an organization through attitudes toward its industry or its specific mission and by the demographic characteristics of the customers and labor force.

4. *The industry* of which an organization is a member affects it by imposing codes of behavior and by the directions in which the industry develops.

5. *Research enterprises* affect an organization by developing new technologies or adapting existing technologies for new problems.

Participants. There are six categories of people and organizations that have a stake in the organization's success:

1. *Customers* receive the organization's products. A business's customers are the individuals and organizations that purchase its products. Government agencies' and nonprofit organizations' customers are the people and organizations that receive products because they are entitled to them.

2. *Owners* are the people and other organizations that acquire a share in an organization and gain or lose depending on its success (where gains and losses may be in terms of money or in terms of satisfaction in the accomplishment of some task). A business's owners are its stockholders. Government agencies' owners are the citizens and organizations whose taxes support it. Nonprofits' owners are the people and organizations that contribute money or effort to help it carry out its mission.

3. *Employees* are the people and other organizations that are paid to work for the organization. In this definition, it may be appropriate to regard a firm to which some business function is outsourced as an employee of the organization rather than as a supplier.

4. *Suppliers* are people and other organizations that provide the goods and services the organization needs to function.

5. *Competitors* are the people and other organizations that seek to provide similar products to the organization's pool of customers.

6. *Bystanders* are the people and organizations that are not directly affiliated with the organization but that have an interest in its activities and the consequences of those activities. For example, the residents of a town that depends financially on the prosperity of a business have an interest in activities that affect the local economy.

The search matrix in Exhibit 1.1 consists of the 35 cells created by crossing the five sectors with the seven categories of participants.

The first step in using the matrix is to search for information that addresses the *current state* of affairs for each cell (e.g., the current level of economic prosperity supporting customer demand and interest rates; current government regulations, tax policies, and support of education; current societal attitudes as well as the age and income distributions in the population; current ability of industry watchdogs to promote good conduct and encourage movement toward industrywide goals; currently available technologies and their ability to meet the organization's needs).

Next you look for *early signs of shifts* in the sectors (e.g., signs of economic slowdown or increase, calls for restrictive or liberalizing legislation, social calm or unrest, an increase or decrease in the birth rate, effectiveness of industry-imposed codes of behavior, reports of potential technological breakthroughs or early tests of new technologies). Then you seek *predictions of significant shifts* in the sectors (e.g., forecasts of runaway inflation, likely shifts in immigration policy, predicted increases in the birthrate, anticipated industry adoption of product safety standards, predicted availability of technology for automated production).

		Sectors				
		Economy	*Government*	*Society*	*Industry*	*Research*
	Customers					
	Owners					
Participants	Employees					
	Suppliers					
	Competitors					
	Bystanders					

Exhibit 1.1   Search Matrix for Guiding Information Procurement in Assessment of an Organization's External Environment

All of this information is written in the cell, and it often is best to phrase (or label) each entry in terms of implied *demands* or *constraints* on the organization. Information that cannot be identified as a demand or constraint may not be relevant and perhaps should be dropped from further consideration. (Note too that whole cells may be irrelevant, but don't dismiss them too quickly. They may have a relevance that you've never considered before.)

The second step in the use of the matrix is to identify the cells for which you have either a paucity of information or information about which you have questions. This helps you direct the search for new information or clarify, confirm, or refute information you already have. The goal is to obtain as complete a picture as possible, a picture that inspires confidence in its credibility.

The third step is to label each demand and each constraint in terms of whether it is a *threat* to the organization, an *opportunity* for the organization, or an *interesting combination*. This analysis sets the stage for thinking about possible courses of action the organization could undertake in order to thwart threats—or turn them to opportunities—and to take advantage of opportunities.

By the way, I prefer to sketch the search matrix on big sheets of butcher paper and hang the sheets on the walls of a conference room. I do this because I want to have a very direct feel about the information and be able to scratch out, draw connecting lines, and generally get involved in a way that helps me form a clear picture of what is going on. Later, the results are cleaned up for transfer to a computer for archiving.

Warning #1: As information procurement proceeds and the matrix fills up, some opportunities and threats may begin to eclipse others. This can lead to premature decisions about the organization's options. Although the more obvious opportunities and threats clearly need attention, it is risky to ignore the others. Subtle threats can turn out to be an organization's ruin, and subtle opportunities can turn out to be its salvation.

Warning #2: It is important to regard the search matrix as a tool, not as a substitute for thought. It can be useful in promoting thoroughness, but it can impose limits too: If something does not fit comfortably within the matrix, it may be ignored. Good sense requires you to be aware of these limits and to think beyond the boundaries of the tool. After all, leadership is granted those who can think broadly; tools are merely aids in that endeavor.

An Example

Before turning to assessment of the internal environment, let us examine how the search matrix can be used in assessment of the external environment.

Background. Recall the little story about Poor Wayne that opened the Introduction to this book. The fictionalized company that Wayne had led so badly is an old firm that we will call "Steller Art Frames," located in a Southwestern American city near the Mexican border, a city in which many people are bilingual and in which many families have strong ties to northern Mexico. The company was founded in the 1920s by a cabinet-maker, George Steller, who began making custom picture frames using motifs from the turn-of-the-century arts and crafts movement in domestic architecture. His frames particularly complemented mission-style furniture and interior design, which had become extremely popular throughout the United States. The designs were especially favored for framing California-school and Southwest art: soft lines, gilded with gold or silver leaf for a mellow, antiqued finish. All of the work was done by hand, and sales initially were to individual artists or by special order through high-end framing shops and art galleries. In addition to high quality, Steller frames were known for never warping and never separating at the corners. This was achieved by a patented fastening technique, invented by Mr. Steller, which kept the frames rigid. Competitors tried to devise similar fasteners but gave up after receiving unpleasant letters from Steller's lawyer.

The business grew over the years as Steller began selling through a wide range of shops and department stores, aided by a steadily growing interest in mission-style decor. Because production was labor intensive, the number of employees had reached 42 when the George Steller died in 1958. George's daughter Beth expanded the business by adding frames imported from Britain as well as a line of mission-style frames made both with oak and with aged wood salvaged from old buildings throughout the Southwest and Mexico. By 1996, the company employed 107 people, fairly equally divided among producing the original frames, producing the new line of wood frames, importing the English frames, and administrative services. An annual catalogue was published, for which requests were received from throughout the world, but little effort was made to expand sales beyond the United States and Canada.

From the beginning, Steller's administrative staff was reasonably stable, but there was high turnover among frame makers. This was because Steller's couldn't afford high wages, so shop employees tended to be young people, usually new immigrants from Mexico who were looking for their first job. In addition to low pay, the work was rather dull and repetitive, so workers moved on when opportunities arose. The result was that the four shop supervisors spent a great deal of time training new workers and monitoring product quality. High turnover was regarded by Beth and the board of directors as Steller's greatest weakness.

Steller had gone along peacefully for years, growing slowly but not actually changing much, making just enough money to meet its payroll, pay its bills, and stay in business. Things began to go wrong when the demand for arts and crafts designs leveled off at the same time that the taxes on Steller's building jumped (it was located in a historic area that was becoming very trendy, making property values skyrocket). The result was that Steller's lost money for the first time since it was founded.

The company clearly was in trouble by the time Beth retired in 2002. The board of directors, most of whom were elderly relatives of the company's founder, hired a manager whom they charged with turning things around. The manager's first reaction was to cut costs, beginning with staff layoffs. Costs indeed went down, but profits stayed flat because the layoffs slowed production and delayed deliveries, leading to a decline in sales as long-time customers were forced to go elsewhere for lower-quality frames. Moreover, the layoffs so distressed the surviving employees that they simply resisted all attempts to make any further changes. Before long things got so bad that the directors were forced to fire the manager and search for a replacement.

Enter, Poor Wayne. Like his predecessor, Wayne was charged with making the company profitable again, and like his predecessor, he immediately began to implement solutions to problems he did not understand. But Wayne's solutions were far more grandiose. He produced a plan that nobody understood or accepted; he offered special discounts to Steller's two best customers, on which he lost money; he bought equipment to automate the gilding of wood for frames, which produced more gilded wood than the framers could use, and the machine gilding was shoddy compared with hand gilding; he partnered with a high-profile chain of picture frame shops to sell rather nondescript little frames under their joint names, which lost money and ended when the chain abruptly pulled out; and he entertained offers to merge with one of Steller's competitors without telling the directors. Exit, Poor Wayne.

Wayne's replacement, Carson, was uninterested in quick fixes and had no taste for grandiosity. More important, she had read this book. She began by learning about the company and its problems, in the course of which she created a committee of employees to conduct an assessment of Steller's external environment, guided by the search matrix in Exhibit 1.1. (Incidentally, the assessment committee's members thought of themselves as "team players" and named themselves "The Mighty Carson Art Players," after a feature on the old Johnny Carson TV show. They found this label humorous on a number of levels, but nobody else did, and it soon was forgotten. However, it resulted in everyone affectionately referring to Carson herself as "The Mighty Carson," a nickname she publicly discouraged but secretly relished.)

The membership of the assessment committee represented a cross section of Steller's employees, people who clearly were influential opinion makers as well as some of the older employees who knew a lot about

Steller's history and the picture frame business. In addition, Carson sent out a notice to all employees asking for nominations to the committee and added two people she hadn't previously considered. Perhaps as important, she asked the board of directors to assign one of their members, ex officio, to the committee to represent the board's viewpoint and to serve as a communication link with the board.

This assessment committee began by examining each of the sectors for each customer category in the search matrix, recording what they already knew in each cell of the matrix. Thus, for example, in the cell for economy/customers they listed Steller's current customers and how the current state of the economy influenced their demand for Steller's products, how perceived short-term and long-term economic trends would influence their demand, and the constraints these placed on Steller's actions.

Then the committee did the same thing for the economy/owners cell in the matrix, with a focus on profits and performance demands. Next they did it for the economy/employees cell, with a focus on employee mobility and pressures for pay increases, both of which posed potential demands on Steller and both of which were threats. The committee proceeded in this manner through participants, suppliers, and competitors. Then they did the same thing for government/customers, which in Steller's case was a vacant cell because there didn't seem to be anything that government was doing or was about to do that would cause customers to stop buying its products. On the other hand, the government/owners cell was important because Steller's owners were distressed by the steady increase in property taxes as their building's value increased. Similarly, the government/employee cell was important because of ongoing proposals at the federal level to change Social Security and because of rumors of federal legislation that could influence employee health care benefits.

After everything the committee members knew was entered into the matrix, they began to search for information to fill in the holes and to confirm or refute what they thought they already knew. In this case, they turned to an experienced information broker who helped them clarify their thinking and to formulate meaningful questions. As the answers flowed in, they reformulated many of their questions and often came up with wholly new ones. After a while, they found themselves with fewer and fewer questions and with all of the cells filled in or identified as irrelevant.

When they were comfortable that they had a reasonably complete picture, they began to assess the demands and constraints in each cell and how these resulted in opportunities and/or threats. Thus, owners' concern about possible tax increases leading to decreased profits was coded as both a demand (taxes must be paid) and a constraint (profits are difficult to increase, and costs can be cut only so much), which pose threats (effects on Steller's already meager profits of paying the increased property taxes and the fact that it would be difficult to pass tax costs on to the customers) as well as opportunities (increasing production and decreasing costs by moving production to a new city-designated enterprise zone that offered low-cost leases on old warehouse space and tax relief in exchange for hiring unemployed youth; moving production 50 miles south to Mexico and taking advantage of tax provisions related to NAFTA, the North American Free Trade Agreement). This suggests a possible scenario in which Steller's six supervisors officially become trainers, with appropriate raises, to create and supervise a workforce either in the enterprise zone or in Mexico. The goal would be to make the training so thorough that product quality could be maintained. Then, by training large numbers of workers (which would keep the trainers busy) and increasing production (which would keep the new workers busy), prices could be lowered to gain a larger share of the existing market. In addition, if new designs were offered, other markets could be accessed, reducing Steller's dependence on mission-style frames.

This scenario raises new questions that require further information search: Are appropriate workers and production facilities available in the zone or in Mexico? Can Steller's supervisors be convinced to become full-time trainers? Can they be taught to teach even better than they do now? Is increased production a good thing? That is, would demand for mission-style frames increase if prices were lower, and how much would sales at the lower price have to increase to compensate for the new workers' wages? For raises for the trainers? Do markets exist for other designs? Would the support staff in the home office have to be increased if production increased or new designs were offered? Would it be possible to meet these increased costs and still increase profits? Are there tax and other NAFTA advantages to moving production to Mexico, and if so, do they compensate for the awkwardness of splitting the company between two geographical locations? Are the advantages of moving to the new enterprise zone sufficient to offset the disadvantages of giving up the building that had been Steller's home for over 80 years and hiring from what might be an unreliable work pool? If the answers to these questions make one or the other of these scenarios tenable, then they are retained as options in the planning process to be described in Chapter 4. If the answers show the scenarios to be untenable, the scenarios should be rejected (or tinkered with until they become tenable) and different scenarios must be sought to deal with the assessed threats and opportunities for each cell in the search matrix.

As you can see, this is not an easy task, but important tasks seldom are easy. Moreover, the matrix is not a perfect tool; it is an aid to thought, but it doesn't replace it. The matrix is merely a framework that helps you keep things straight as you go about the search for information about the external environment and as you interpret that information in terms of the threats and opportunities it reveals. Recall our metaphor of the external environment as a playing field. The purpose of being in the game at all is to play well enough to survive and prosper. The strategy for doing this is to understand the demands and constraints of the playing field and how they threaten or provide opportunities for your team to advance toward its goal. But, you can't begin to advance until you know where you are on the playing field and in which direction you need to move in order to reach the goal. Additionally, even if you know in which direction to move, you can't figure out how to do it unless you know your team's strengths and weaknesses. Knowledge of strengths and weaknesses is gained by assessing the organization internal environment, to which we now move.

(A final note to our story: The people Carson put on the assessment committee worked together so well and did such a good job that she asked them to stay on to do the internal assessment. This, in turn, worked out so well that the assessment committee became the vision committee (Chapter 3) and then, with a couple new members, it became the planning committee (Chapter 4). But a new group took over when it was time to implement the plan (Chapter 5) because the members of the old committee were worn out. All of this is very hard work.)

Assessing the Internal Environment

An organization's internal environment consists of its purpose, its efforts to differentiate itself from competitors, its component functions, the organizational structure within which these functions operate, how authority and power are distributed and exercised, and the values and beliefs that constitute the organization's culture.

All of these can be changed if changes are called for as a result of identifying opportunities and threats in the external environment. The ease and success of attempting to make changes in all the others, however, rest on making changes in the culture. This is because all the others are enmeshed in the culture, and changing them requires making concomitant changes in the culture, which often is difficult. Because culture and culture change are so important, Chapter 2 is entirely devoted to them. Therefore, in what follows, we will concentrate on assessment of other aspects of the internal environment and then move on to a more detailed discussion of culture in Chapter 2.

Documents

Assessing the internal environment often is easier than assessing the external environment because leaders frequently have a background in the industry and they frequently have moved up through the organization they are leading or one very like it. This experience is invaluable because it provides a core of information to which assessment information can be added. Moreover, there usually is a vast supply of written documents pertaining to the organization: annual reports, brochures, internal memos, policy statements, and records. Although some of these documents are little more than propaganda, it is possible to learn from them, if only how the organization attempts to present itself. Careful reading can yield information about the organization's products, customers, employees, board of directors, business strategy, organization structure, and its financial state. Greater detail can then be obtained by talking with people in the various functional areas of the organization (e.g., accounting, marketing, production, human resources).

Purpose. Every organization exists for a purpose, usually summed up in a mission statement. Generally, an organization's mission statement is accurate, insofar as the people who wrote it understood what the organization actually does. Sometimes, however, the statement's authors had a limited view of the organization, and the mission statement is therefore limited. For example, the mission statement for a famous company said that it was in the restaurant business. Then someone pointed out that it actually owned and operated only a few restaurants. Most of its revenue came from franchising, leasing shop space to its franchisers, and providing supplies to those same franchisers. Recasting the mission statement to emphasize that the company was primarily a franchising business with capabilities in managing property and supplying food and other products prompted recognition of previously unconsidered opportunities. Similarly, in an example to be described in Chapter 3, a charity hospital that always had defined its mission as providing health care for the poor found that it was only by providing care for paying patients that it could afford to continue doing charity work. Recognition of this broader mission led to changes that saved the hospital from closing.

The lesson here is that leaders can learn from their organizations' mission statements as part of the appraisal of the internal environment, but it is unwise to be limited to what the statements say.

Differentiation. Most organizations operate in a competitive environment, whether they are businesses that compete for customers, government agencies that compete for tax dollars, or nonprofit organizations that compete for donations or grants. Each must find a way to differentiate its products from those of its competitors in order to attract the resources they need to survive. Exactly how they differentiate depends on what they perceive to be their products' strengths vis-à-vis competitors': quality, availability, efficiency, beauty, exclusivity, innovation, novelty, value for money, ethical superiority, moral rightness, or some other characteristic that is important to those who control the needed resources. For example, discount stores differentiate themselves from department stores by offering brand name goods at lower prices. In fact, some low-cost merchants boast that they will not be undersold, lowering their prices below those of other low-cost merchants in an effort to make sure that what differentiates them from their competitors remains intact. In contrast, makers of luxury products differentiate on quality and exclusivity; quality is a claimed attribute of the product, and exclusivity is ensured by charging so much that ownership is limited to those few who can pay for reputed high quality. Even when products are not particularly different, advertising can produce the illusion that they are. Relief agencies, for example, compete in helping poor children in Third World countries advertise on American television in the hope that name familiarity will increase their share of charitable donations.

Functions. Every organization must distribute tasks among its members. In a small organization, a few members may share in the tasks, with one or the other taking primary responsibility. Larger organizations need more formal task assignment, if only so members will know where to go to get what they need to do their jobs. This leads to creation of units within the organization that have exclusive responsibility for a particular area of the organization's activities. Thus we see production, finance, accounting, marketing, human resources, and product development assigned to different units, each overseen by a manager who reports to higher management. Each of these units may have its own internal subunits; the human resources departments will have subunits for hiring, for benefits, for training, and so forth.

Structure. The structure of an organization consists of the way in which its various functional units relate to each other. This often is depicted in an organization chart; boxes represent units, and lines represent the reporting relationships among them.

There are some five or six prototypical structures for organizations; what is "best" depends on the organization's purpose, its size, and the characteristics of its external environment. This is not the place to go into more detail; textbooks on management (e.g., Robbins & DeCenzo, 1998) discuss it under the rubric of organizational structure or organizational design.

Authority and power. Authority and power are not exactly the same. Authority comes with the job and often includes power, but power sometimes exists outside the organization's formal structure. Authority can be traced by examining the organization chart. In the typical hierarchical organization, the president or CEO is at the top of the pyramid; the vice presidents of the various divisions are at the next level; the managers of departments are next; the managers of the subunits in the departments are next; and the rank and file is at the bottom. The degree of hierarchy differs from one organization to another, but the structure of most is some variation on this classical form. To the degree that hierarchy prevails, the lines of authority are clear; the people at each level receive orders from the level above, translate them into actions appropriate to their unit, and transmit orders about these actions to the level below them.

Authority is downward and accountability is upward. Accountability means that performance of assigned tasks is evaluated by the authority on the next higher level of the organization, who then administers rewards or penalties. Accountability, which justifies performance evaluation, is intrinsic to a hierarchical organization structure. Accountability often is less clear in organizations that have less hierarchical structure.

The power that accompanies authority and the ability to reward or punish is often called *coercive power* (or *reward power* or *legitimate power*) because it derives from subordinates' fear of reprimand, dismissal, demotion, penalties, or absence of rewards. Although the term is more pejorative than it probably needs to be, coercive power often makes subordinates do things that they might prefer not to do. This is not necessarily bad if it is used to serve the best interests of the organization and its various stakeholders, but the potential for abuse is obvious.

Because both authority and coercive power tend to be vested in relatively few people in the organization, these few people have an immense influence over the working lives of everybody else. This imbalance of power in organizations mirrors a larger imbalance in society, an imbalance that has incited everything from the foundation of trade unions, to experiments in socialism and communism, to revolutions and civil wars. At issue is how to balance the virtues and drawbacks of authority-backed coercive power—especially in business and government—against the virtues and drawbacks of broad participation in deciding how that power will be used and how the resources it controls will be distributed. This struggle underlies the debate about centralized versus distributed government (Washington vs. the states and the states vs.counties and cities), as well as issues about totalitarianism versus democracy, command economies versus demand economies, and so on. Many of the milestones of history reflect this struggle (e.g., the Magna Charta, the American Civil War, and the disintegration of the Soviet Empire). The balance between coercive power and participation has been the major drama for at least the past three centuries and shows no sign of abating. Indeed, it underlies almost any conflict you can name, on the global level, on the national level, locally, and in virtually every organization, large and small, public and private.

In the business arena, the power-participation issue within organizations has come more sharply into focus as service industries become an increasingly large part of modern economies. Some businesspeople, and some academic theorists, have proposed that service organizations might work best if the usual hierarchical structure were turned upside down. The frontline members of the organization would be at the top as befits their importance as the people who encounter the customers and deliver the service. Every level of management below them would exist primarily to support them. The CEO would be at the very bottom, the ultimate provider of support for the entire organization.

The inverted hierarchy is a pretty idea; it has value in emphasizing the importance of frontline people in service organizations; and it may even make a difference in how some organizations think of themselves and how they conduct business. But merely turning the organization chart upside down does not change the fact that the power hierarchy is right side up, with the CEO at the top, because the ultimate power to reward lies with the CEO. On the other hand, inverting the structure prompts recognition of a particularly important truth: leadership has two seemingly conflicting roles in organizations: (a) to control and direct through wise use of power and (b) to support and enhance the actions of the frontline people. The paradox of power is that in order to do their jobs well, leaders must simultaneously direct and serve those whom they lead.

There is a subclass of coercive power that derives from the organization's structure but which does not rely upon the authority that this structure engenders. This is the power deriving from the ability to bypass the formal structure of the organization in order to get things done quickly and efficiently. The prototype is the administrative assistant who has risen through the ranks with all the other administrative assistants and who can accomplish the impossible with just a phone call. This ability to use friendships and swap favors gives the person enormous local power; everyone around him or her comes to depend on this power to cut through bureaucratic red tape. Indeed, the more hierarchical the structure, the more bureaucratic the organization tends to be (in the bad sense of bureaucratic), and people who know shortcuts can be extremely powerful. Again, this kind of power can be very valuable, but it also can be abused, especially when there is favoritism in who is granted access to it.

In contrast to coercive power, which sometimes prompts people to do things they do not want to do, *persuasive power* prompts people to want to do them. Coercive power is granted by the organization to its leaders, but persuasive power is granted by those who would be persuaded. Persuasive power derives from other people's belief that an individual is informed, well intentioned, trustworthy, unbiased (or at least has the "proper" biases), and not out solely for personal gain. Such individuals can be anywhere in the organization, exercising their persuasive powers on their coworkers, either formally or informally. Formal persuasive power might be exercised by a particularly popular and trusted shop steward. Informal persuasive power might be exercised by an ordinary worker who has the courage to speak out against abuses or in favor of newly introduced policies that he or she thinks are beneficial. These people often exert such strong effects on employee opinion that they must be taken into account by the formal power structure; leaders do well to know these people and what they think and, where possible, to work through them. Better yet, leaders should conduct themselves in ways that result in their being granted persuasive power by organization members.

Walk Around

Documents can provide only so much information about the internal environment of an organization. This must be fleshed out—made into something living and vital—by getting to know the people in the organization and what they do. A great deal of this kind of insight is gained simply by walking around and talking with people at each level of the organization. This sort of inquiry, however, must be done with care; the problem isn't so much who you talk with as who you don't talk with. People may be leery of talking to "the Boss," but they will be far more upset if the Boss talks to others and not to them, or to their subordinates and not to them. This means that you need a strategy that will show even-handedness but that will get the information you are seeking. It is a good idea to know all your managers, if you possibly can, and to talk with their subordinates after you have talked with them.

Everybody likes to talk about their job. The problem is keeping them on track so they actually tell you what they do and what it contributes to the organization (or at least to their unit). In the course of this, you can learn what they see as the organization's purpose and how they envision the organization's present and future. Of course, the questions you ask must not be too leading, but you don't want to get bogged down in gossip or end up with a litany of complaints (although you can learn a lot from both). The problem with listening to gossip and complaints is that the former often is bad information and the latter comes with the expectation that you will do something to remedy things. The point of doing a walk around is to learn about the organization, not to receive bad information or build expectations that you may be unable to meet.

A walk around should include each functional unit of the organization, both line functions and support functions. Many leaders find line functions, such as production or distribution or sales, more interesting than, say, accounting or human resources, because they so obviously contribute to the organization's mission. The support functions, however, are equally important and must be understood. Organizations get into trouble more frequently from financial and personnel problems than from inability to produce decent goods or services.

Finally, your walk around should proceed beyond the immediate confines of the organization. If there is a board of directors or an advisory board, you should take time to talk to each member, asking them much the same questions you asked people in the organization. Then you should try to get to know the leaders of competing organizations; they will have opinions about your organization and about the external environment in which your organization and their organizations compete. You cannot collude with them, but you need not be personal enemies simply because you are competitors.

In some sense, the local community is as much a part of the internal environment as the employees are, if only because the employees and their families live in the community. Therefore, you should seek out community leaders at various levels to see how your organization is viewed locally. Many highly respected organizations are hated by their neighbors for failure to contribute positively to the community. In some cases, this local animosity makes it difficult to hire good people or be treated evenhandedly by local government or other community organizations. I once consulted for a company that had so outraged the community that its employees' children were harassed by schoolmates and job vacancies went unfilled because people were unwilling to be identified with the company. One service worker told me that in the old days he had been greeted as a hero when he arrived to make repairs, but now he was treated as though he were personally responsible for there being a problem in the first place. He had stopped telling new acquaintances where he worked.

What to Look For

Your inspection of documents and your questions as you meet with people in the organization should address both specifics about their jobs and generalities about how the organization works. The following is a partial list of these generalities, although there will be others for any particular organization:

1. Do members believe themselves to be a part of the organization or merely being employed by it? If the latter, are they merely marking time until they can leave, and where will they go?

2. Do members believe themselves to be part of a team or merely a member of a unit, responsible for only their own duties?

3. Do members believe they are encouraged to be innovative and entrepreneurial in how they do their jobs? Do they believe that their ideas get a sympathetic hearing and that they are recognized appropriately for their contributions?

4. Do members believe that performance is fairly evaluated?

5. Do members believe that rewards and penalties are fairly distributed and accurately reflect actual contributions to the organization?

6. Do members believe that conflict within the organization is handled well by management?

7. Do members believe that authority and power are used to further the proper interests of the organization or to control for control's sake?

8. Do members believe in the effectiveness of existing channels through which decisions can be appealed or complaints made?

9. Do members believe that management decisions take into consideration the impacts on subordinates, their families, and the surrounding community?

10. Do members believe that management adequately understands the external environment?

11. Do members believe that management adequately understands the internal environment?

12. Do members believe that management adequately understands the changes that must be made in the external and internal environments in order to address threats and take advantage of opportunities?

To be continued . . .

Discussion of internal assessment won't be complete until we have examined the organization's culture in detail. In the course of walking around and asking questions of employees, however, you'll begin to get a clear picture of the culture (organizational beliefs and values) and the climate (whether employees are generally satisfied or dissatisfied with the organization and how things are going). Climate changes over time as a function of good and bad things happening, but culture is robust, changing slowly unless prompted to change. As we shall see, culture can be an obstacle to change or it can promote it. When it is an obstacle, and when changing is crucial to the organization's fortunes, culture change becomes a priority. In Chapter 2, we will discuss the nature of culture and how it can be changed when change is required.

But first . . .

Before we move on to Chapter 2, let us return to our fictionalized company, Steller Art Frames, and some of the results of its assessment of its internal environment. The gist was that Steller's long-time employees were found to be extremely loyal to the company and that they understood that as things stood at the moment, the company was likely to fail and that something substantial had to be done if failure were to be prevented. However uncomfortable it made them to think of change, they were willing to cooperate with any reasonable measures to save the company and their jobs. They were concerned, however, that efforts to turn things around might compromise what they saw as the company's greatest assets: the high quality of its products and the pride they took in their work. Moreover, they were afraid that changes would result in Steller's becoming a less satisfying place to work, especially if it were to get larger. They felt that their input could help shape changes, but most of them felt they lacked the wisdom to know what those changes should be. They looked to The Mighty Carson and the assessment team for guidance, withholding judgment until they better understood the nature of the threats and opportunities the company faced and until a new vision was presented for the company's future. Many employees confessed to a deep unease about the future, whether the company tried to ride things out by sticking to the status quo or tried to reinvent itself to meet its challenges. They simply were waiting to see what happened next.

A significant discovery during the internal assessment was that Steller's patented fastening system was more versatile than previously thought. One of the perquisites of being a senior frame maker was the use of Steller's shop and its tools for noncommercial projects on the weekends. In the course of the internal assessment, one of the frame makers told the committee that he had used Steller's fasteners on some furniture he had built for his daughter's twin sons. These extraordinarily rambunctious boys had used the furniture for 3 years and, aside from scratches and dents, hadn't been able to harm it. This prompted Carson to have Steller's lawyers make sure the company had a solid lock on the fastener system, with an eye to licensing it to furniture makers and creating another income stream for Steller.

Summary

To ensure mastery of the foregoing material, summarize it for yourself it by filling in this topic outline.

Assessment: Specifying Change

I. Assessing the external environment
   A. Buying information
   B. Walk around
   C. Where to look
      1. Sectors
      2. Participants
      3. States
   D. The search mix
   E. What to look for

II. Assessing the internal environment
   A. Documents
      1. Purpose
      2. Differentiation
      3. Functions
      4. Structure
      5. Authority and power
   B. Walk around
   C. What to look for

Exercises

1. Arrange* to interview a current or retired leader of a medium-to-large for-profit, nonprofit, or governmental organization. Prior to the interview, write each question you want to ask at the top of a clean sheet of paper and then take notes on his or her answer in the space below the question. Questions should focus on each of the topics discussed in this chapter (e.g., external and internal environmental assessment, differentiation, power, participation). At the close of the interview, seek permission to return with further questions. (Future interviews will focus on the topics in each of the chapters following this one.)

2. Arrange* similar interviews with people—either currently working or retired—at other levels of the same or a similar organization. This should include officers of the organization other than the president or CEO (i.e., department heads, supervisors, team leaders). Contrast their

answers to your questions with those given by the leader and the other interviewees.

3. Write a short essay on the results of your interviews in an attempt to integrate what you have learned into a personal viewpoint about leadership at different levels of organizations.

4. Place this and future essays in a notebook to create a record of your views about leadership and organizational change.

* If you do not know anyone suitable, ask your instructor or the alumni coordinator of your institution for suggestions and a letter of introduction.

Sources and Further Reading

Anderson, D. V. (1985). *Illusions of power.* New York: Praeger.

Beyer, J. M., & Browning, L. D. (1999). Transforming an industry in crisis: Charisma, routinization, and supportive cultural leadership. *Leadership Quarterly, 10,* 483–520.

Choo, C. W. (2001). Information management for the intelligent organization: The art of scanning the environment (3rd ed.). Medford, NJ: Information Today.

Conger, J. A., & Kanungo, R. N. (1998). *Charismatic leadership in organizations.* Thousand Oaks, CA: Sage.

Deeds, D. L. (2003). Alternative strategies for acquiring knowledge. In S. E. Jackson, M. A. Hitt, & A. S. DeNisi (Eds.), *Managing knowledge for sustained competitive advantage.* San Francisco: Jossey-Bass.

George, W. (2003). *Authentic leadership.* San Francisco: Jossey-Bass.

House, R. J. (1976). A theory of charismatic leadership. In J. G. Hunt & L. L. Larson (Eds.), *Leadership: The cutting edge* (pp. 189–207). Carbondale: Southern Illinois University Press.

Klein, G. A., Orasanu, J., Calderwood, R., & Zsambok, C. E. (Eds.). (1993). *Decision making in action: Models and methods.* Norwood, NJ: Ablex.

Kotter, J. P. (1990). *A force for change: How leadership differs from management.* New York: Free Press.

Leavit, H. J. (2003). Why hierarchies thrive. *Harvard Business Review, 81,* 96–102.

Mintzberg, H. (1975, July-August). The manager's job: Folklore and fact. *Harvard Business Review,* 49–61.

Northouse, P. G. (2004). *Leadership: Theory and practice.* Thousand Oaks, CA: Sage.

Robbins, S. P., & DeCenzo, D. A. (1998). *Fundamentals of management.* New York: Prentice Hall.

Rost, J. C. (1991). *Leadership for the twenty-first century.* New York: Praeger.

Sutcliffe, K. M., & Weber, K. (2003). The high cost of accurate knowledge. *Harvard Business Review, 81,* 74–82.

Weber, M. (1947). *The theory of social and economic organizations* (T. Parsons, Trans.). New York: Free Press.

Weinberger, D. (2001). Garbage in, great stuff out. *Harvard Business Review, 79,* 30–32.

Two

Culture: Constraining Change

*Prime Responsibility #2: Leaders must work
with others in the organization to understand the organization's
culture: the core beliefs and values that are shared by the organization's
members, that guide their actions in its behalf and define their expectations
about the actions of those around them. If the culture impedes progress,
they must work with others to change the culture appropriately.*

Authentic leaders strive to understand their organization's basic values and beliefs because they know that values and beliefs shape how the organization's members interpret events, including the leader's words and actions. They know that misinterpretation of even the best intended words and actions leads to resistance and, in the extreme, to outright rebellion. The first step in understanding values and beliefs is to watch the organization in action, which will reveal many things in addition to routine task-related activities. Careful observation will reveal a pattern of ceremonies, conventions about how to dress, use of jargon, ways of acknowledging status, shared standards for doing various jobs, and frequently recited stories about how the organization came into being and how it has dealt with various crises. Further observation, and a little reflection, will show you that all of these features of the organization actually are only surface manifestations—artifacts, if you will—of an underlying core of fundamental values and beliefs that are shared by the organization's members. These shared standards for determining what is true, right, appropriate, proper, necessary, desirable, or unthinkable—for the organization and about how one ought to act in the context of that organization—are called the organization's culture.[1]

Because it is shared, and because it lies at the heart of what they do and think, the organization's culture provides its members with a common viewpoint that binds them together as a group. It helps them understand the activities of others in the organization, and it guides their own activities within and on behalf of the organization. Because the culture embodies what is desirable and undesirable—how things should and should not be— it dictates the kinds of activities that are legitimate and the kinds that are not legitimate. Thus the culture not only places constraints on activities of the organization and its members (cultural prohibitions), it also prescribes what the organization and its members *must* do (cultural imperatives). In short, the culture guides the activities of the organization and its members.

What Culture Does

An organization's culture:

1. Defines what is of primary importance to the organization, the standards against which its successes and failures should be measured;

2. Prescribes how the organization's resources are to be used, and to what ends;

3. Establishes what the organization and its members can expect from each other;

4. Makes some methods of controlling behavior within the organization legitimate and makes others illegitimate; that is, it defines where power lies within the organization and how it is to be used;

5. Dictates the behaviors in which members should or should not engage and specifies how these are to be rewarded and punished;

6. Sets the tone for how members should treat each other and how they should treat nonmembers: competitively, collaboratively, honestly, distantly, or hostilely; and

7. Instructs members about how to deal with the external environment: aggres- sively, exploitatively, responsibly, or proactively (from Harrison, 1972).

In short, the culture is the essence of what is important to the organiza- tion. As such, it prescribes and proscribes activities; it defines the "dos and don'ts" that govern the behavior of its members.

Cultural Artifacts

Even when an outsider understands and appreciates the culture of an organization, its artifacts sometimes appear a little silly. It often takes a little probing to understand why people take them so seriously and how they relate to the group's core culture. In fact, their major function is to serve as constant reminders to the group members about what is important.

Clothing and jargon. When, as a business college professor, I started doing executive education and business consulting, I was amused that business- people tended to dress so formally and use so much in-group jargon. In fact, I once went to a meeting at which everyone, without prearrange- ment, showed up wearing blue blazers and black shoes; all of the men wore gray trousers and all of the women wore gray skirts. I recall thinking that it must be difficult to live in such a conformist world. A few days later I attended a faculty meeting. When I looked at my colleagues and myself, I was equally amused. Our clothes conformed to the informal, genteel scruffiness that is the hallmark of academia, and our in-group jargon was even more obscure than that used by the businesspeople.

The careful formality and special language of the business world and the studied informality and equally special language of academe both sig- nal belongingness and seriousness. In both cases, the members conform in order to affirm to themselves and others that they share the beliefs and values of their respective cultures. In the case of the business people, these tend to be order, success, and purpose. In the case of the academics, these tend to be a feeling of separateness from (and perhaps just a little superi- ority to) the broader society and high regard for interesting, clever ideas.

Rules to break. Culture not only sets rules to be followed, it sometimes sets rules to be broken, and in breaking them, the members affirm an under- lying shared belief. For example, I once was a visiting professor at an ancient and highly respected European university. On the first day of class, I arrived early, prepared to begin precisely on time. In contrast, the students only began to arrive at the time the class was scheduled to begin, and they continued to wander in over the next 15 minutes. I attributed this tardiness to it being the first day, but I became increasingly dismayed as it happened day after day. At first I thought I must be mistaken about the scheduled time, but I wasn't. Finally, when I couldn't take it any more—all this lateness offended my American need for punctuality—I asked the students what was going on. I was cheerfully informed that coming to class up to one quarter of an hour late was a time-honored tradition at that university. Bemused, I asked the regular faculty about it and was assured that it indeed was a tradition. As they explained it, this calculated tardiness was viewed as a way for the students to assert themselves and to flaunt the bureaucracy. In short, the culture set the rule about the time at which class began, then it legitimatized breaking that rule; but it imposed a 15-minute limit on how severely the rule could be broken, all in order to affirm the cultural belief, shared by faculty and students alike, that university students are mature people who are responsible for their own behavior and who are not slaves to bureaucratic formalities and timetables.

Founder stories. The Nike athletic shoe company built its initial success on a unique feature, the "waffle sole" of its running shoes. The story about how this sole came to be reached almost mythic proportions within the company. It seems that Bill Bowerman, one of the company's founders, put a sheet of rubber in a waffle iron and stuck the resulting crinkled sheet of rubber to the bottom of a pair of running shoes. The traction and cushion the rubber provided was a revolution in athletic shoes. The much-retold story itself came to underscore Nike's cultural belief in innovation, experimentation, and the importance of being on the cutting edge of product development.

Similarly, the J. C. Penney Company long revered its stories about its founder and namesake. Mr. Penney's first stores, started in 1902, were called Golden Rule Stores because he believed in treating his customers according to the golden rule, "Do unto others as ye would have them do unto you" (Matt. 7:12; Luke 6:31), a belief that remained central to the company's culture through many changes of fortune and of business strategies. Many organizations have such founder stories (McDonald's Ray Kroc, Wal-Mart's Sam Walton), sometimes as much myth as truth, but always illustrative of something of cultural importance. As is the case with other artifacts, the stories serve to remind the organization's members about important cultural beliefs, to reaffirm the belief's prominence in the culture, and sometimes to provide a hero after whom employees can model their behavior.

Nonconformity

Although some cultural conformity may be contrived and mere pretense, for the most part it is not. Group members usually feel much more comfortable when their behavior is appropriate to the group's norms and mores. Like the businesspeople and academics previously mentioned, they willingly dress in the prescribed manner, and as in the case of the European students, they honestly feel more independent and self-assertive when they arrive at class a little late (but not too late).

Consider what would happen to the nonconformist in either setting. A businessperson who consistently shows up at sales conferences in scruffy clothes or an academic who always shows up at committee meetings in a suit is making a statement, at least in the eyes of other group members. The statement is that he or she is different from everyone else in the group, that he or she does not share the same norms and regards the other folks' norms as of so little consequence that he or she is not bound by them. In short, an individual's failure to comply with the norms is taken as a declaration that he or she is an outsider. Outsiders get treated as outsiders: They're isolated or ejected from the group.

The Origins of Culture

People form groups that subsequently grow into organizations in order to do something. For start-up businesses, that something usually is to explore an economic opportunity, although there often are other motives such as independence to run one's own enterprise or merely the excitement of doing something new. For other kinds of organizations, the motives are quite varied. Zander (1985) found that of 72 new nonbusiness organizations, 18 were formed to promote social change, 14 were formed to produce some product, 13 were formed to reform some other organization, 11 were formed to change the members themselves, and the remaining 16 were formed for more specialized purposes.

Values and Beliefs

A new group is founded for a specific purpose, whether to become a business, a social club, a self-help group, or something else. As the group gets off the ground, its members begin to engage in the activities that they perceive to be necessary to accomplish the purpose for which it was formed. At this point, the purpose alone is the goal of these activities, and the purpose alone defines what activities are or are not appropriate, although there may be a great deal of flailing around and hit-or-miss activity until the members learn what produces progress and what does not.

As the members begin to learn ways of successfully promoting the group's purpose, they begin to catalogue what they have learned so each lesson will not have to be learned repeatedly. The catalogue may be informal and passed on from one member to another by word of mouth. For a small group with a very specific purpose, this informal arrangement may be sufficient. If the group begins to grow, however, formal guidelines may have to be developed, perhaps in the form of bylaws for internal governance and lists of standard operating procedures for dealing with recurring problems and tasks.

Development of Culture

Formalization of activities to serve the group's purpose is a major step in the journey from being a loose-knit group with a few dreams to becoming an organization with a real culture. Other steps, however, take place prior to and concurrent with it. Early on, members begin to evolve beliefs and values about how to interact with one another and with people outside the group. Although they are seldom written down, these institutional ethics are very strong and very influential. Violations are met with escalating degrees of disapproval by other group members and, in the extreme, can result in expulsion from the group.

Together, the formal and informal rules about what to do and how to behave in the group start to take on a life of their own. They may begin as simple statements about the activities of group members, but they evolve into something more, something quite powerful. As it becomes clear what's expected of the group's members, and as the group's purpose becomes more explicit, there develops a sense among the members of "who we are, what it is that we do, and how we do it." In short, the rather straightforward purpose and activities that characterized the group in its infancy give way to more sophisticated conceptions. With this change come a sense of group identity and, quite simply, the beginnings of a culture.

Activities

The activities of the group members as they pursue their various jobs also contribute to the growing culture. In turn, the emerging culture begins to influence the activities. That is, as the culture develops, it clarifies which activities are valued and which are not. Actions that might have got by in the early days are now seen as unacceptable. Actions that might have been neglected are now seen as desirable, perhaps even mandatory. A two-way relationship develops between activities and culture, each shaping the other and each making the other sharper and clearer.

As the organization matures and begins to develop a culture, its activities become differentiated. *Tactical activities* are directed at very concrete, immediate goals, for example, hiring someone to fill an open position or serving on a committee to plan a social event. *Operational activities* are directed at somewhat longer range goals, for example, restructuring office procedure to decrease delays in the processing of orders or conducting a membership drive for a community theater. *Strategic activities* are directed at long-range goals that shape the organization's future and what it will become, for example, entering a new market or broadening the range of charities supported by a foundation.

Tactical goals are seldom ends in themselves; rather they contribute to achievement of operational goals. So, too, achievement of operational goals contributes to achievement of strategic goals. Thus, strategic activities are "bundles" of operational activities, which in turn are "bundles" of tactical activities. Indeed, an observer would never actually see operational or strategic activities, because they are abstractions. All he or she would observe would be tactical activity, because this is the level at which physical action, actual behavior, takes place. Behavior does not occur for its own sake; rather it is guided by higher-order considerations: what it is aimed at accomplishing. The higher-order considerations are the operational goals and, ultimately, the strategic goals. Therefore, because they give direction to everything that is done, the ultimate strategic goals, and the intermediate operational goals that contribute to attainment of the strategic goals, are central to the thrust and scope of the activities within the organization.

This differentiation among tactical, operational, and strategic levels of activities and goals is very important in understanding concepts presented in later chapters of this book.

Unified and Fragmented Cultures

As the group becomes bigger, it develops the trappings of an organization: a name, perhaps a logo, and a differentiated structure, with each part having a specialized function. The original culture that served all of the members in earlier times becomes less serviceable as the group becomes an organization. Now each division, perhaps each unit in each division, evolves its own subculture (how we in the shipping department uniquely do things and why). In the best of all possible worlds, however, each of these subcultures encompasses at least some part of the larger organizational culture—perhaps its primary elements—in addition to the unit's own unique characteristics.

Unified Cultures

To the degree that the different subcultures in an organization each include a set of similar elements, we can speak of the organization's culture as being unified, or strong. This is not to say that the common ground among the subcultures is always what the organization's top leaders think it should be; that is quite another matter. Rather, the common ground, the overlap among the subcultures, as it actually is, constitutes the organization's overarching culture. This means that overarching culture is not necessarily dispensed at the top of the organization to seep down to the lower levels. The organization's leaders may think that this is how it works, and they may think that if they try to change the culture from the top, it necessarily will change throughout the organization, but they usually are wrong. It is much more difficult than that to change culture. The reason it is difficult, of course, is that the culture is embedded throughout the organization as part of each subculture, and it is a major job to change each of those subcultures.

Drawbacks. It might seem like a unified culture is vastly to be preferred to a fragmented culture, but that is not always true. A unified culture means that, to some degree, everyone in the organization sees things in the same way because they share the same set of beliefs. Unfortunately, when this happens, the organization may become extremely rigid. Even if it understands how to cope with threats to the organization, leadership (i.e., you) may meet extreme resistance to necessary changes. ("That's not the way we do things here!") Instead, the organization's members may prefer to continue doing what has worked for them in the past, maybe even doing more of it, although it is inappropriate and ineffective in the current situation. When an organization does this in a competitive environment, it may be overtaken by its less rigid competitors.

It is important to remember that even a unified culture is not wholly homogeneous; subcultures exist and each division or unit in the organization sees things from a slightly different perspective. D.C. Dearborn and his colleague, the Nobel Prize winner Herbert Simon, had executives from a single company read a case study that was to be discussed as part of a training program. Before the discussion began, they asked the executives to write down what they each saw as the primary problem facing the organization described in the case. As one might anticipate, the head of marketing saw the problem as a marketing problem, the head of finance saw it as a finance problem, the head of production saw it as a production problem, and so on. That is, the different heads of the different divisions in the company tended to view the world in a way that was congruent with their own division's function, and in terms of the culture that their division had evolved. This is not to say that they did not share parts of each other's culture, but they did have views unique to their own parts of the organization.

Fragmented Cultures

When subcultures do not share much common ground, we speak of a fragmented, or weak, culture. Here each subculture is substantially differ-ent, and the members from different subcultures are marching to differ-ent drummers. This is not always bad. Consider a research laboratory in which each scientist pursues his or her own projects; the role of manage-ment is merely to hold things together and to provide the resources so each unit can get on with its work.

Drawbacks. Often, however, a fragmented culture is a sign of an organiza-tion that is coming apart, its various units each fending for themselves without any feeling of mutual dependency and without the synergy that cooperation and community can generate. The real drawback of a frag-mented culture is that, lacking a solid core of shared beliefs and values, there is no foundation on which to build efforts to move the organization if it encounters trouble. A unified culture that becomes rigid will resist change, but trying to change a fragmented culture is like trying to herd cats.

Cultural Change

It would be a mistake to think that just because culture shapes activity and activity tends to reinforce culture, that culture always becomes rigid and unchanging. Perhaps this would happen in a vacuum, but most organiza-tions are buffeted by developments in their external and internal envi-ronments that make change inevitable. The question is how to manage change: Is it best to go slowly, allowing the organization's members to adapt in stages, or to plunge ahead, risking resentment and resistance?

Organizations instigate change—both in what they do and in their cultures—in response to threats and opportunities. The following are some of the most obvious and universal:

Economic crises. The effects of economic crises on organizations are familiar to all of us. Steep increases in interest rates make borrowed money more expensive and cause organizations to delay or cancel expansion. Inflation can eat up profits or make raw materials prohibitively expensive. Worker demands for increases in pay or health care coverage, however reasonable, can push a company to the edge. We all have seen firms disappear when they could not cope with economic changes, often because their cultures simply did not allow for appropriate responses and their leadership lacked the skill to change the cultures to fit the new conditions.

Laws and regulations. We also have seen the effects of new laws, of new or amended regulatory rulings dictating how organizations must operate, or in some cases of deregulation of industries and the ensuing scurry for competitive advantage. For example, when laws regarding hazardous waste disposal came into being, most firms tried to be socially responsible and meet the new demands. Some were unable to afford the expense and went out of business. Others found ways around the laws, at least for a time. In every case, the laws required changes in how companies dealt with hazardous waste disposal, with consequent threats to their economic viability as well as to their cultures. Of course, one person's threat may be someone else's opportunity: New companies sprang up to dispose of hazardous waste for other companies and a whole new industry was born.

Social change. Changes in society also confront organizations with threats and opportunities. Many firms resisted the growing antismoking sentiment in the 1980s on the grounds that it was too much trouble to segregate smokers from nonsmokers. Legal and social opinion, however, soon became so strong that a few companies took steps to eliminate smoking in the workplace. These pioneering firms soon found they saved money on insurance and sick leave, so they became even more zealous in their efforts. Similarly, the recent interest in low carbohydrate food has proved troublesome to some businesses but provided new business opportunities for others. In another vein, widespread outrage about excessive executive pay has led many businesses to be more circumspect (and more creative) in how they compensate their leaders. So too, public outrage about scandalous misuse of corporate funds, Enron for example, has led to changes in the rules defining acceptable accounting practices, causing many businesses to restate their earnings for recent years and to change the ways in which they present themselves to the investment world.

Demographics. The changing demographics of both its customers and its members also pose threats and opportunities for an organization. When the country has an abundance of young people, things youthful become important, organizations tend to adopt a "with-it" image for their services and products, and their cultures come to reflect the beliefs and values that are important to their predominantly younger members. At other times, when the relative number of young people is low, organizations and their services and products become more conservative and come to reflect the beliefs and values of their predominantly older members (who, by the way, may be the same people as before, only older and more mature). For example, as the members of a social club become older and more affluent, the purpose of the organization may change to accommodate its members. It might become more exclusive so that membership is a sign of having "arrived," or it might become more philanthropic, using the energy it once devoted to parties to doing good works in the community.

Internal crises. A change of key personnel can be a major turning point for an organization. New people bring their own ideas and styles, and these often conflict with the existing culture. Indeed, frequently the major reason for replacement of key people is to produce changes in the organization and its culture, but the crisis this produces should not be underestimated. Similarly, power struggles among different coalitions of key people can lead to internal crises that challenge the existing culture, with the victorious coalition having to win the culture over to its procedures and goals.

Evolutionary Change

There is a story told, and it might even be true, about an American tourist visiting the garden of one of England's stately homes. Clearly overwhelmed by the beauty of her surroundings and desiring to plant something like it when she got home, she asked a nearby gardener how one went about creating such an exquisite garden. The gardener paused and then replied, "First, you start 400 years ago."

If you examine the histories of older, well-established organizations, you find that through all their ups and downs; through the comings and goings of leaders; through crises and changes in the economic, political, and social environments in which they operate; nearly all of them demonstrate a steady, unhurried pursuit of one or two key goals. Assuredly, they have gone through many changes in response to threats and opportunities, they have succeeded in some things and failed in others, but they kept at it. Indeed, some of them are so plodding and dull to the outside eye that they scarcely arouse interest. But, they are survivors in a world in which most new organizations fold within a year or two. And if they are businesses, they are considered safe investments that make money but that probably will not make you rich.

Many of these long-lived organizations have fairly placid environments, so the threats they generally face are not dire. Others have tempestuous environments but have cultures that thrive on challenge. In either case, they have evolved to fit their environmental niches, and their cultures reflect this evolution. Moreover, they often have a history of reasoned evolutionary change that has purposely shaped them to accommodate the kinds of changes that occur in their respective environments. In each case, the assumption seems to be that what the organization will be required to be in the future is an extension of what it is now, not a wholly reengineered, completely different organization. The trick is to figure out what that extension is and to evolve in the proper direction without unduly disrupting the organization's operations.

Evolutionary change means that change occurs over a reasonably long time, but this does not mean lethargy or foot-dragging is tolerated. Even in the middle of major changes, minor changes must be made to address arising needs, and people must be convinced to accept these little changes just as they need to be convinced about the big ones.

Usually the motivation for evolutionary change is a broadly defined threat such as structural shifts in an industry or in social trends that will change consumer tastes or eventuate in legislation affecting the organization's products or services. When people throughout the organization understand the threat, and its likely timetable, they usually become motivated to consider how the organization should react. If plausible reactions run afoul of the organizational culture, people must decide if they care enough about the organization's survival to countenance the cultural changes necessary to accommodate the proposed reactions to the threat. If they think accommodation is too high a price to pay, they usually abandon the organization, either as individuals or as a group. More likely, they will try to find a middle ground that will allow them to salvage the most important aspects of the culture while changing other aspects so they can address the threat.

Revolutionary Change

Cultures evolve and change in even the most peaceful times. But they tend to change rapidly in times of trouble because, whatever other beliefs the culture may prize, it usually prizes survival most of all. Economic crises, changes in laws or regulatory rules, rapid social changes, demographic trends, internal crises, and many other events influence what the organization must do to survive, and the culture tends to change accordingly. This is not to say that the culture is totally flexible and subservient to external pressures: Sometimes organizations die rather than make changes that negate or violate the beliefs that comprise their cultures. More often, however, they try to keep as much of their culture intact as they can while bending enough to survive. In this they are not unlike individuals who try to be moral and ethical and stand up for what they believe but who often must compromise when the crunch really comes. They may not break, but they certainly bend.

Revolutionary change tends to be far more difficult for existing leadership than for new leadership. This is because the existing leadership often has itself absorbed the organization's culture and has difficulty even conceiving of anything but minor modifications of the status quo as solutions to the organization's problems. Top management's inability to abandon the past and propose bold changes is merely human. Few of us are able to make abrupt departures from what is familiar and comfortable. In the leadership of organizations, however, this can be dangerous, and it often prompts a cry for new leaders. It is standard practice in industry to replace old leaders with new ones when a radical change in direction is necessary. Similarly, the need for "new blood" in government is a familiar electioneering slogan.

Some degree of change is nearly always expected with new leadership, either a single leader or a whole new team. In part, this is because the new leadership wants to make its mark and establish its authority. To signal that it is doing so, it institutes various changes. In part, changes in leadership were brought about because the organization was in trouble and the former leaders were either unwilling or unable to meet the challenge.

Change as a fad. Evolutionary change tends to be disparaged in the popular business literature and on the seminar circuit. Prevailing wisdom is that the business environment changes so quickly that only draconian, revolutionary measures can induce the organizational changes necessary for survival. The excesses produced by this viewpoint are readily apparent: hastily introduced innovations, massive reorganizations, excessive "downsizing," rapid sales or purchases of assets, and companies branching into businesses they do not understand. In short, businesses in particular and organizations in general have endured wrenching changes, many of which, in hindsight, seem to have been done more for the sake of change than for any sound business reason. In many cases, far less is accomplished than is promised. True, some businesses are ripe for reorganization or need to change the mix of their workforce, but many go far beyond what is necessary, instituting grandiose restructuring, wholesale firings, and early retirements. After the blood stops flowing, it often is found that all the misery and turmoil had little positive effect on the bottom line—in either the short or long term—and that the newly reduced workforce is too small to keep up with demand, necessitating overtime and a constantly stressed staff. The initial savings inflate reported profits, but this peters out quickly.

In large part, this ideology of revolutionary change on the part of businesses (and other organizations such as universities, which seem to have caught the disease from business) was brought on by rapid economic growth followed by recession. Because they often focus only on the short run, leaders seem to forget that the economy ebbs and flows and that booms and recessions come and go. The trick, of course, is to skillfully weather the bad times without weakening the organization so much that it cannot recover and prosper during the good times. Evolutionary change takes place too slowly and seems infuriatingly sluggish to leaders who are in a panic about the organization's stock price or its ability to survive the crisis that is immediately at hand (or who want to make their mark and move on). For the most part, however, there is more time than leaders think there is; Armageddon is seldom as near as it seems; and although the pace can be quickened in times of crisis, slower more reasoned change is most likely to work, causing less long-term damage to the organization.

The Key to Change

An organization's culture functions primarily to keep it doing what it already is doing. (This is true even when the culture believes in constant change, in which case it will resist efforts to slow or stop change or, unfortunately, to steer change in a new direction.) The larger the organization, the more the culture fosters the status quo and the harder it is for leaders to instigate revolutionary change, even when most members recognize that desperate times require desperate measures and that the status quo is no longer feasible.

For both evolutionary and revolutionary change, the key lies in changing activities first and then allowing the culture to adapt. This means that the focus, rather than being on the culture itself, must be on getting the organization's members to accept changes in their routine activities and the immediate goals of these activities. Revolutionary change in both activities and culture differs from evolutionary change primarily in terms of its urgency. Revolutionary change has less time for participation by the members in formulating the changes, and it is less tolerant of the need for assurance about reversals if the changes do not work out as expected. It generally is motivated by arguments for doing something now, doing something big, and doing something permanent!

Instigating Change

The success of attempts to instigate change is dependent on the situation. At one extreme, members will go along with the leadership's (your) proposed changes in activities if these changes don't violate the organization's existing culture very much. Indeed, if there is fairly high congruence between the proposed changes and the culture, that congruence, although imperfect, may argue for accepting the changes and cooperating in their implementation. At the other extreme, if members are fully convinced that the status quo is doomed and that the whole enterprise is going to founder if something is not done, they may go along with the proposed changes, even if they violate the culture, simply because the culture will not matter anyway if the organization dies. There are, of course, degrees between these two extremes, situations in which the members know that things are not going well and that something must be done, but your proposals are not sufficiently congruent with the culture and certainly will eventuate in basic changes in the nature of the organization.

Minor change. Look first at the case in which the proposed changes require members to do things that are only slightly incompatible with the existing culture. Here the first task, aside from deciding what must be done, is to convince them that there is a need for minor changes by pointing out that present and foreseeable conditions are slightly incompatible with what they believe and value and that something, however small, has to be adjusted to bring about compatibility. Having established the need for minor change, the second task is to demonstrate how the proposed change solves the problem while leaving the culture almost wholly intact. The third task is to promote acceptance of the changes, perhaps provisionally, so that their effectiveness can be tested—"Let's try it this new way and see how things go."

Done with any degree of sensitivity, this process usually works because all (you and the members) are in agreement from the beginning about what is important and inviolable in the culture. The important feature of the proposed changes in activities is that although they may be revolutionary, they are only slightly incompatible with the culture, they are not the usual way things are done, but they are not so much at cross-purposes with the culture that they are rejected out of hand. The threat to the culture of not doing anything motivates a willingness to accept minor changes, although they may not exactly fit with the culture; the danger of not accepting them often is that the threat will increase. Of course, there will be debate in the hallways and at the watercooler about whether these particular changes are the best ones, about whether the threat could not be met just as well with activities that do not stress the culture; but things usually can be worked out because nobody is adamantly resisting the change on principle.

Major change. In contrast, even when members can be convinced that the threat is huge and the foreseeable future is vastly incompatible with the culture, proposed changes that are strongly incompatible with it still are going to meet with resistance. This resistance is not necessarily born of malice, although leaders often view it as such. Rather, resistance is prompted by the threat the proposed changes in activities pose for the culture, which, after all, embodies the things the members value about the organization. Remember, violated expectations tend to promote anger. The proposed activities may be viewed by some members as a default on what they see as an implicit contract; that is, it is your job to preserve the organization and now what you propose to do threatens the organization's fundamental nature. The result may be rebellion, either overt or covert.

Overt rebellion comes out in confrontations at meetings, arguments in the parking lot, or even in strikes. Covert rebellion comes out in discontented gossip, slowed productivity, increased turnover, turf wars between units, reduced coordination of activities, and a general sense of dissatisfaction. Overt or covert, obstructers often can severely weaken your leadership or bring it down simply by bringing the organization's activities to a stop.

When you see that the changes you propose will significantly violate the existing culture, you really have only three avenues open to you. First, you can get tough, unilaterally impose mandatory changes, and then pick up the pieces afterward. Second, you can try to convince the members that the crisis facing the organization is so large that it justifies activity that violates the culture and that may change the culture profoundly. Third, if time permits, you can make smaller changes in activities so that the culture at least begins to spiral away from the present culture toward the new culture the organization needs, saving more far-reaching changes for later on. Each avenue has its strengths and weaknesses.

If the crisis facing the organization is acute and there is little time to spare, mandating change unilaterally may be the only avenue open to you. Even if things are not so pressing, you may judge the long-term gains of the proposed change to be worth the price exacted by imposing those changes, but the price is often steep. If other organizations are open to them, members who strongly identify with the existing culture may leave. Their skills may be missed, but on the other hand, their positions in the organization can be filled with new people who may be more sympathetic with your aims. If leaving is not practical, these members may decide to fight the changes, and the ensuing strife can badly weaken the organization. Moreover, it is not at all certain that you will be the winner. Of course, if you lose and the proposed changes turn out to have been necessary, everyone loses. This is a very risky way to introduce change.

The second avenue, convincing members that the crisis is so pressing that cultural violations are acceptable, is also risky. It is a two-edged sword. First, in order to convince the members, you usually have to frame your arguments in terms of present or potential threats to what is important to them, the existing culture. On the other hand, that very culture is violated by the changes that are being proposed. It is not unlike the famous quotation from the Vietnam War, "In order to save the village, we had to destroy it."

Arguing that culturally unacceptable changes are provisional may convince some members, but it will not convince them all. It may take a little time, but people will come to realize that even these provisional changes begin to erode the culture, and expediency is a dangerous path if one believes strongly in the principles embodied in the culture. To take another example from the national level, internment of Japanese Americans during World War II was a severe violation of American cultural values in the name of protecting the culture. As it turned out, the internment caused far greater problems than it addressed, not the least of which was violation of the Bill of Rights.

Or, consider how universities have come to encourage faculty members to commercialize their research discoveries, providing both the universities and the researchers shares in the resulting enterprises. Critics think that although this policy affirms the universities' belief that more money is always needed, it erodes the more fundamental belief that the research and discovery should be motivated by intellectual curiosity and the disinterested search for knowledge rather than the opportunity for personal gain.

Clearly, it is risky to use the culture to justify proposals that might change that culture. On the other hand, if the crisis facing the organization is so great that its culture is bound to change even if it survives, its members may decide that survival outweighs their scruples about the change in activities. When situations like these arise, all but a dissenting minority will, with varying degrees of enthusiasm, permit violation of the culture, accept the proposed changes in activities, and wait to see what happens. Of course, taking this route does not mean that everything necessarily will turn out badly. In fact, the changes in culture that result from changes in activities may be exactly what is needed, and somewhere down the line the members may actually thank you for your foresight and for persisting in the effort to promote the changes. At the time, however, radical change, perhaps correctly, looks suspicious and tends to trigger resistance and distrust.

The third avenue for instigating change in an organization is through small changes in activities that change the culture in small steps, eventually leading to the large changes that the organization supposedly needs. This takes time. Assuming, however, that you are convinced that changes are necessary to the organization's survival and success, then this third avenue usually holds the most promise for reduced resistance and, eventually, successful change.

The Bottom Line

Finally, we come to the secret of how to decide on the changes that an organization needs—both evolutionary and revolutionary changes—and how to get members to accept those changes. The secret is in having a vision of what the future culture will look like, what the organization will become, and what the benefits for everyone will be for undergoing the stresses and strains of changing. Vision, therefore, becomes the key. I will describe this key role of vision in the next chapter.

Summary

To aid in mastery of this material, summarize it for yourself by filling in this topic outline.

Culture: Constraining Change

  I. What culture does
    A. Cultural artifacts
      1. Clothing and jargon
      2. Rules to break
      3. Founder stories
    B. Nonconformity

  II. The origins of culture
    A. Values and beliefs
    B. Development of culture
    C. Activities

  III. Unified and fragmented cultures
    A. Unified cultures
      1. Drawbacks
    B. Fragmented cultures
      1. Drawbacks

  IV. Cultural change
    A. Evolutionary change
    B. Revolutionary change
      1. Change as fad

  V. The key to change
    A. Instigating change
      1. Minor change
      2. Major change
    B. The bottom line

Exercises

1. Return to the current or retired leader you previously interviewed with questions about the role of organizational culture in facilitating and resisting change. Also ask the person's views about how culture comes to be and how it evolves. Inquire about the degree to which his or her

organization's culture is unified or fragmented and what the implications are for leading the organization. Ask about how the culture has had to change to fit changing circumstances and how that change came about.

2. Return to the other leaders to whom you spoke earlier and pose the questions described above.

3. Write a short essay that describes your current viewpoint about organizational culture and add the essay to your notebook.

Note

1. The Organizational Culture Inventory in Appendix B can be used to obtain a quick-and-dirty snapshot of an organization's cultural values.

Sources and Further Reading

Beck, R. N. (1987, February). Visions, values, and strategies: Changing attitudes and culture. *Academy of Management Executive, 1,* 33–41.

Bernick, C. L. (2001). When your culture needs a makeover. *Harvard Business Review, 79,* 53–59.

Beyer, J. M. (1981). Ideologies, values, and decision making in organizations. In P. C. Nystrom & W. H. Starbuck (Eds.), *Handbook of organizational design.* New York: Oxford.

Bjork, L. G. (1985). The function of cognitive images in facilitating organizational change. *Journal of Human Behavior and Learning, 2,* 44–55.

Charan, R. (2001). Conquering a culture of indecision. *Harvard Business Review, 79,* 75–82.

Dearborn, D. C., & Simon, H. A. (1958). A note on the departmental identification of executives. *Sociometry, 21,* 140–144.

Gordon, G. G. (1991). Industry determinants of organizational culture. *Academy of Management Review, 2,* 396–415.

Harrison, R. (1972, May-June). Understanding your organization's character. *Harvard Business Review,* 75–85.

Meyer, A. D. (1982). How ideologies supplant formal structures and shape responses to environments. *Journal of Management Studies, 19,* 45–61.

Pitman, B. (2003). Leading for value: A CEO-led transformation of a company's culture. *Harvard Business Review, 81,* 41–46.

Sathe, V. (1983, Autumn). Implications of corporate culture: A manager's guide to action. *Organizational Dynamics,* 5–23.

Trice, H. M., & Beyer, J. M. (1991). Cultural leadership in organizations. *Organizational Science, 2,* 149–458.

Zander, A. (1985). *The purposes of groups and organizations.* San Francisco: Jossey-Bass.

Three

Vision:
Motivating Change

> *Prime Responsibility #3: Leaders must work with others*
> *in the organization to create a vision, a reasonable story about the*
> *organization's future in light of the constraints imposed by its environment*
> *and culture, and to articulate the goal agenda that follows from that vision.*
> *Then they must promote acceptance of the vision throughout the organization.*

In Chapter 2, we saw that as an organization grows, the relationship between its activities and its culture becomes more complex. In addition to "what we do" and "what we believe in," a sense of direction begins to develop: "what we want to become." This sense of direction, the agenda the organization perceives itself to be pursuing, is its vision. Thus, activities, culture, and vision become an interrelated whole, each interacting with and shaping the other within the context of the organization's external and internal environments. Culture embodies the organization's fundamental beliefs and the imperatives that are dictated by these beliefs. Activities flow from these imperatives, but they also influence the imperatives and the beliefs that give rise to them. Vision defines the ideal future, perhaps implying retention of the current culture and the activities, or

49

perhaps implying change. That is, the vision may require no more than natural evolution of the present, or it may require radical changes in what the organization is doing and in its culture in light of trends, threats, and opportunities present in its external and internal environments.

What the Vision Isn't

The Vision Isn't the Mission

Many organizations confuse their organization's vision and its mission. Worse, they presume that a mission statement is the statement of their vision. They are wrong.

The vision is a narrative, a story that tells the organization who it is now and who it ideally will be at some time in the future. That is, the vision helps members understand what the organization is now and what it is striving to become. In contrast, the mission describes what the organization does—its activities—in pursuit of the goals dictated by the vision. The mission derives from the vision.

People often presume that because they have concocted a mission statement that they therefore have created a vision. I use the word *concocted* because mission statements that do not derive from a vision tend to be mere verbiage, a collection of jargon and catch phrases that neither inform nor inspire. Most organizations that start their search for a vision by writing a mission statement never develop a true vision because the brief mission statement promotes a narrow mind-set. It makes about as much sense to write a mission statement in the absence of vision as it would to write an executive summary before you write a document; in both cases the tail wags the dog by exerting a powerful and limiting influence on what is, after all, the main event.

The Vision Isn't a Plan

People often confuse vision with plans. True, the organization's vision is a story about a desirable future that implies an agenda of goals, which, in turn, implies plans for attaining them, but the implied plans usually are quite vague. Eventually, concrete plans will have to be made, and concrete actions will have to be taken, but the vision itself seldom outlines either of them very precisely.

Although the vision is not the same thing as a plan, it gives rise to and dictates the shape of plans. The vision sets the goals, and the plan maps the path to those goals in light of environmental constraints. Without planning (and implementation), the vision remains an abstract dream. Without the vision, planning (and implementation) tends to focus on solutions to short-term problems. The vision infuses the plan with energy because it gives it direction and defines long-term objectives. Even the most unassuming vision challenges the organization to become something stronger, better, different. It is a glimpse of the future's potential. As such, it is a mixture of reality and imagination.

The Vision Isn't Just for Threats

People often think that a vision (and planning and implementation) is solely to address threats. In fact, opportunities also require a vision in order to make the most of them. Opportunities are circumstances that, if properly utilized, can lead to outcomes that satisfy the organization's cultural values, just as threats are conditions that can lead to outcomes that violate those values. For example, a firm that is going along nicely may see a new product or a new market as an opportunity to do even better, thus satisfying its cultural imperative for growth and success. In contrast, a firm that is in danger may see leaving its current business and entering another one as an opportunity to save itself, also satisfying its cultural imperative for growth and success *and survival*. Recall the rather optimistic old saying, "There are no problems, just opportunities."

The Vision Isn't Necessarily Dramatic

History provides examples of dramatic visions that have inspired productive action and bettered the lot of those who were inspired by them. Visions offered by, among others, Winston Churchill, Franklin Roosevelt, John F. Kennedy, and the "I Have a Dream" speech by Martin Luther King Jr. at the March on Washington in 1963 are dramatic in their sweep and inspiring in their eloquence. They are more notable than most workaday visions because they are movingly stated and they address changes of magnificent proportions. But for all that, they are fundamentally the same as the vision that every organization needs to motivate necessary change and give direction to its actions. Every vision helps its intended audience recognize things they perhaps already know but have not put into words: who we are and who we want to become.

Elements of the Vision

By now I hope you are convinced that to avoid trouble or to seize opportunity, the organization needs a creative vision to guide it. The good news is that the process of building that vision is not particularly mysterious.

A vision has four elements: goals, priorities, requirements, and implications. Seldom does the vision contain very fine detail about each of these elements; that will be spelled out in the plans that derive from the vision.

Goals

Goals are the most important elements of vision. They are the stars, and the other elements are the supporting players. Goals have two attributes: thrust and scope. *Thrust* is the direction that vision prescribes for the organization. *Scope* is the breadth of the undertaking and the comprehensiveness of its impact on the organization's culture and activities, and it is dictated by the comprehensiveness and magnitude of the thrust. Together thrust and scope constitute the vision's goals, the future toward which the organization should strive.

Priorities

Priorities give differential weight to the goals and add a time dimension for their accomplishment. Some goals are more important than others; some must be attained first if the others are to be attained subsequently; and some are tangential to the real thrust but are necessitated by cultural considerations.

Requirements

Requirements for achieving the vision often center on anticipating the skills and tools that might be needed to reach its goals. One of the reasons for failed vision regularly cited by managers is that although the organization's members accept the new vision and work hard to achieve it, they lack the required skills. Sometimes this means that the vision must include retraining programs. Sometimes it means the vision must include ideas about recruitment of new people who possess the requisite skills. Sometimes it means the vision must include tasks being done by people outside the organization. All of these will cost money, so another requirement is that the vision must include a realistic idea about how things are going to be paid for.

Implications

Implications of failing and succeeding are the final element of vision. Failure can be disastrous, and although they may not be fleshed out, the vision should at least suggest fall-back positions. On the other hand, success that is followed by awful surprises can be just about as bad, and it too needs fallback positions. Risk is part of being alive, but risk can be reduced, if only a little, by attempting to anticipate what might happen if efforts fail and if they succeed. For example, without a fallback plan, the firm that dreams of independence and security by ridding itself of debt and amassing a large cash reserve may be setting itself up for a takeover. Vision that is heedless of the possible negative implications of both failure and success is asking for trouble.

Sources of the Vision

Vision is not the unique gift of a few special leaders who, because of their extraordinary foresight, are singularly adept at leading ailing organizations out of the darkness and into the light. There is no denying that some leaders do a better job than others of communicating their particular vision to the organization's members. There is no reason, however, to believe that their sense of vision is necessarily superior to anyone else's (recall that Adolph Hitler was a particularly gifted communicator).

The fact is that what often is cited as almost clairvoyant, nearly messianic vision is usually recognized as such only in retrospect. When a leader's vision proves spectacularly successful, both the leader and the successful vision become bigger than life and are accorded a special place in the organization's mythology. The myth attributes exceptional powers to the leader who, without that striking success, would probably be regarded as just an ordinary person. Notice that one seldom hears failure hailed as visionary, even when the fault was in planning or implementation and not the vision. The truth is that vision is less special and more mundane than many would like to think.

Leaders' Vision

Whatever our doubts about charisma, we must not summarily dismiss the vision that strong leaders present their organizations. Especially when the leader has a good track record, his or her vision often is very influential. In the 1980s, when stepping down after 14 years as a programming executive at NBC television, Brandon Tartikoff expressed fear that nobody at NBC had a vision of what they wanted the network to become. He contrasted this with the clear vision that Grant Tinker had brought to NBC when he took over as chairman 10 years earlier, bringing NBC's shows to the top of the ratings.

"The vision was, we're going to try to get the best producers, give them the greatest freedom, encourage them to bring us their projects of passion, and give them what no one else gives them, which is time to connect on the air with the audience and let the audience catch up with some of their shows" (quoted in Shales, 1991).

The result was that shows that were slow starters were allowed to stay on the air until they found their audiences. Although neither would comment, it was broadly believed throughout the industry that both Tinker and Tartikoff left NBC because this vision no longer prevailed. After General Electric bought it in 1981, NBC was subjected to stringent cost cutting, a shift in emphasis from quality to profit as the measure of success, and a marked decline in morale and in NBC's desirability as a place to work. As often happens when the control of an organization changes hands, the ensuing clash between the new and the old cultures and visions made some people quit rather than compromise their beliefs and dreams.

Members' Vision

Just as it is a mistake to think that vision arises from the special talent of gifted leaders, it also is a mistake to think that it *only* arises from leaders, gifted or otherwise. Like culture, vision belongs to everyone in the organization. That is, each member has his or her own vision for the organization, although any particular example may be rather idiosyncratic and heavily focused on its owner's own future in the organization. Usually, however, the members' private visions contain some sense of the larger organization's future, if only because a common culture underlies them. To the degree that each individual member's vision is congruent with the vision of the other members and with leadership's vision, we can speak of consensus about the organization's vision.

Consensus

Growth of consensus about a vision means that what were once unconventional ideas about the organization's future become conventional.

Although there are many different visions within an organization, most of them receive little attention, and only one or two emerge as the contenders for adoption. Sometimes the survivors are the visions of one or two people, but quite often they seem to arise from somewhere deep within the organization. Although it would be interesting to know their origins, the most pressing question is why some survive and others die.

It is not difficult to identify key characteristics of surviving visions. They must address identifiable problems, and they must not be markedly incompatible with the culture and activities. The question, however, goes beyond even these basics, for some visions that possess these qualifications still fail to survive. Clearly, there are political considerations that prevail over the mere quality of the vision.

Let us assume for a moment that we have three or four very acceptable, contending visions of an organization's future. They all address the problems that the organization faces, and they all are sufficiently compatible with the culture and current activities to permit them to be considered further. Which one will become the vision that is favored by the members of the organization?

This question, or at least a very similar question, has received close attention from political scientists who study how issues become part of the public agenda. As it turns out, much of what they have learned in the public realm is instructive about how an organization's agenda—its vision—arises from its leaders and from within the ranks of its membership.

Surviving. Milward and Laird (1992) examined the natural history of various issues that aroused public concern and that eventually were acted on by one or another legislative body. They discovered a pattern in the careers of these issues that involves relevance, sponsorship, and timing.

First, the issue must be relevant. It must address the problems that are important to people and contain the rudiments of a solution. It helps if some villainous source of the problems can be identified: a person or organization that is responsible, preferably if their motivation is questionable and what they are doing victimizes innocent people (and we all like to think we are innocent people). The counterpart in a business might be something like the loss of a big contract to a rival firm, which turns everyone's attention to the problem of competing with this obviously malevolent opponent and sets the scene for thinking about how the organization might be able to do better in the future.

Second, the issue must have sponsors. A highly credible person must champion it, and a group that is seen as knowledgeable must push it.

Third, timing must be right. The issue that fits the mood of the moment will have the best chance of surviving to be considered further. The mood may change, but unless the change is large, the issue may remain viable. An issue that is raised before its time will fall on deaf ears; one that is raised after the mood has passed will sink into oblivion. Timing is everything.

Substituting the word *vision* for the word *issue* in the above implies that to have staying power, a candidate to become the organization's vision has to fit the problems that members perceive the organization to be facing, must receive support and endorsement from powerful people and factions within the organization, and must be proposed and discussed at the right time. The further lesson to be learned from political science, however, is that a vision that achieves this consensus still may not be the best vision, just as the vision that comes from leadership may not be the best one. Even if it were possible to identify and clearly label the best vision, it might not turn out to be the survivor.

As you might have gathered from all of this, the odds are slim that a truly good vision is going to spontaneously arise from within an organization, survive the political gauntlet, and achieve the consensus that is necessary for it to become the rallying point. That is why leaders are wise to keep their eye on the competing visions that are floating around within the organization and to help those that have the best chance of addressing the organization's long-term problems and of gaining consensus. Indeed, building on a vision that has its roots in the organization itself greatly improves the chances of attaining consensus.

Evolution and Revolution Revisited

As we saw earlier, there are two modes of cultural change: evolution and revolution. As one might expect, these two modes derive from very different underlying kinds of vision: evolutionary vision and revolutionary vision.

Evolutionary vision sees the future as a natural evolution of the present. This does not mean that things are static. It merely means that as the organization considers what it wants to become, it strives to keep the vision as compatible as possible with its existing culture, only making changes as required and even then focusing on slow and measured changes.

Revolutionary vision sees the future as a profound departure from the present, usually as a result of existing or looming crises. This kind of vision prescribes rapid and radical changes both in how things are done and in the culture that legitimizes those activities.

Each kind of vision, evolutionary or revolutionary, is appropriate in some circumstances and inappropriate in others.

Evolutionary Vision

Books about organizational change often start with the assumption that all organizations are constantly on the brink of disaster. As a result, leaders are exhorted to be a "fireball," to impose revolutionary changes, and to turn the organization around. Lack of change is equated with stagnation. It sometimes seems that proactive is equated with hyperactive.

The fact is, for most organizations most of the time, it is appropriate for the vision merely to be an informed and reasonable extension of the present. If there are no looming threats and participants (including, for example, shareholders, if it is a business, or voters, if it is a unit of government) are satisfied with what is happening, continuing with the present agenda may be in order; the vision may be merely to improve quality steadily, to work on reducing costs or whatever. Change exacts a price, and when change is not needed, an evolutionary vision requiring quiet progress may be best. Contrary to management lore, sometimes the best advice is, "If it ain't broke, don't fix it."

Revolutionary Vision

On the other hand, if the organization is in trouble, or if serious threats or compelling opportunities loom on the horizon, maintaining the status quo may be either dangerous or foolish. If leadership is ever going to be a "fireball," this is the time. The trick, of course, is recognizing and understanding the threat or opportunity and having the creativity to build a vision that can deal with it adequately.

Adequacy of the Vision

The most obvious criterion for judging the adequacy of the vision is whether it addresses the opportunities and threats in the organization's external environment. But that may not be enough. Unless there is a willingness on the part of both leaders and members to endure profound change, a vision that is in direct and irresolvable conflict with the culture and with current practices is not an adequate vision. Similarly, unless it includes a remedy, a vision that requires strength where the organization is weak is not an adequate vision. And, a vision that is implausible or has little chance of success is not adequate. In short, not just any dream will do: It must be grounded in reality, or it's a waste of time.

An adequate vision lies somewhere between mundane problem solving and idealistic dreaming. It sets an agenda that possibly might not be reached but that is so close to being attainable that it inspires the attempt to achieve it. It is this quality of being within the organization's grasp, but requiring serious effort, that allows the vision to inspire, motivate, and unify the organization's members. The most adequate vision is one that addresses the issues and is attainable, but is a challenge.

Two Examples of Vision Building

To see how real organizations build visions, let us examine two examples. The first is a newly founded fire department in a suburb of a medium-size city. The second is a well-established urban hospital located near the center of a very large city. Both found themselves faced with the need to build an effective vision that their various constituencies could support. The second example is particularly instructive because it describes how the vision guided planning and subsequent action, which provides a segue into Chapter 4 where we will discuss planning.

The First Example: A Suburban Fire Department

Southwest Fire Department (not its real name) was formed when the board of a fire district decided not to renew its contract with a private provider, a large emergency services corporation, and set up its own fire department. The district's five fire stations serve a rapidly growing population of about 70,000 residents and 1,000 businesses in an area of roughly 70 square miles. Many of the firefighters previously worked for the fire corporation, and they generally were pleased by the change in employment. As part of its development, the new fire department sought to build a vision that could give a sense of unity to its members and provide direction for its growth (Weatherly, 1995).

The first step. The process began with a series of focus group meetings and interviews with key members of the organization. A fundamental split quickly became apparent: The fire marshal remarked that, "There is no honor in putting out a fire that could have been prevented." Immediately, one of the firefighters replied, "Firefighting is always honorable." As the discussion progressed, it became clear that the group did not share a common view about the reason the organization existed. Some contended that the department's purpose was to prevent fires, and others contended that it was to fight fires, but they all agreed that they were in the "fire business." As it turned out, however, this was not strictly true. Observation of their activities revealed that fire prevention and firefighting were only part of what they did. They provided emergency medical services, collected toys for children, provided safe "haunted houses" for Halloween, helped senior citizens with plumbing emergencies and similar problems, removed wild animals from people's yards, and rescued domestic animals. In short, their real business appeared to be both emergency and nonemergency community service.

Other themes emerged, most of them defined by what the department was not rather than by what it was. Most notably, it was not like the former corporation that provided fire protection. When asked to define what the department was, most members responded by contrasting it with the corporation. Indeed, the culture was more of an anticulture, in that it had no substance other than being different from the corporation. As a result of trying to be different from the corporation (which perhaps had been overorganized and overcontrolling), the department's culture appeared to be fragmented with little integration across the five fire stations and not much better within each station. Indeed, this fragmentation (the feeling that things were out of control and falling apart), previously had prompted moves toward unionization in an attempt to provide a sense of security and organization.

All of this was compounded by the fact that the corporation, for which many of the firefighters had previously worked, was aggressively seeking contracts with areas adjacent to the district's boarders in an attempt to "land lock" the district and prevent its expansion, thus limiting its financial base. The result was a strong sense of threat and the feeling that the department was fighting for survival, although nobody had a coherent idea about what to do to remedy things. The discomfort level was high and the resulting bickering and turf battles were leading to valuable resources being squandered and long-time friendships being destroyed.

Clearly a strong vision was needed to provide a common cause and a viable way of assuring the future of the department.

The second step. While the focus groups and interviews were being conducted, all of the firefighters in the five fire stations were administered the Organizational Culture Survey (Appendix B). The results showed the department's culture to be weak on *reward* and, as you might expect, on *communication, fairness, enjoyment,* and *innovation.* On the other hand, the culture was strong on *achievement, competitiveness, resourcefulness, judgment,* and *integrity.* This suggests that the culture was clear about doing a good job externally, but it was less clear about internal matters such as treating employees well or providing them support for doing their jobs.

A second finding of the survey was that the department had a more unified culture than it at first appeared. This meant that the culture was a better foundation for building a vision and formulating a strategic plan for the department than had been anticipated.

The third step. To augment the results of the focus groups, interviews, and the Organizational Culture Survey, various of the department's internal documents were reviewed, documents that had previously been prepared by outside consultants. For example, one was an assessment of opportunities and threats with suggestions for a strategic plan. Another was the results of an environmental assessment project with recommendations about the implications for the department's future.

The fourth step. A picture began to emerge from the documents, the focus group, the interview information, and the Organizational Culture Survey results. The firefighters were fiercely loyal, but they defined their department in terms of how it differed from the corporation for which they had previously worked. As a result, the department had no distinct identity of its own and was floundering because it had no sense of direction. In short, the department was strong in many ways, but there was no shared vision of where it was going and what it was striving to become.

The fifth step. Armed with all of this information, a task force was formed to create a vision for the department. Following the procedures outlined earlier in this chapter, the task force crafted a detailed document describing the values of the department and the implications for the department's future. By this point, the vision focused broadly on the department's community service rather than only on fire prevention and firefighting. Prevention and readiness to fight fires were retained, but they were not seen as the only goals toward which the department should strive: The department also was envisioned as working toward greater integration into the community. Retention of the traditional elements of the firefighter professional ethos enabled more conservative members of the department to buy into the vision without feeling threatened. Together with the new elements, this made the vision broad enough to be encompassing but narrow enough to provide a basis for sensible planning and coordination of future activities.

The sixth step. A follow-up about a year later revealed that the vision was still in place, that it was in fact driving activities, and that there had been a marked decrease in internal conflict and discomfort with the department. In fact, the first steps had been taken toward formulation of a long-term plan to guide the department's future growth and development.

Some of the comments obtained during the follow-up are instructive enough to warrant inclusion, and they provide a nice ending to our little story:

> We were doing all these programs, but we really didn't know why. It seemed like people were saying, "Hey, this is a great idea; we ought to do this Toys for Tots program." And our leader would say, "Sure. Do it." We didn't really see how it tied to anything. But going through this process showed us that we were doing things right. Focusing on our values allowed us to think a little bigger in terms of our vision. It helped us see how the things we do fit together and serve a larger purpose.

Or,

> We are a caring organization, and we participate in an enormous amount of social service that has to do with the peace of mind of people in our community. When little Mrs. Johnson falls down, and she's not really hurt (and she knows she's not hurt) or she might not have even really fallen down, but she calls us because she's lonely, we've got to talk to her and try and find organizations that can find somebody for her to talk to. We're not saying we're going to be in the counseling business, but what we are saying is we try to be in the referral business.

And,

> Our vision is more than putting out fires. We're really there for our customers' peace of mind in areas we can affect: fire, medical, and a variety of community services.

As is clear in these quotations, the line between vision building and planning is not well defined. As the vision becomes clearer, the outlines of a plan for achieving it also become clearer, a fact that also is illustrated by our second example of vision building.

The Second Example: An Urban Hospital

Mercy Hospital (not its real name) is owned and run by an order of Catholic nuns who founded it in the early 1900s as a charity hospital. Located at the edge of the downtown core, Mercy plays a major role in the care of the city's poor. As was true for many hospitals, Mercy long had financed its charity care by charging its paying patients more than their care actually cost, charges that usually were paid by private or public health insurance. As a result of pressure from insurance companies and from programs like Medicare, however, the margin that paying patients contributed began to be reduced. Because charity cases were never turned away, the institution found itself underwriting their care, resulting in increasingly serious financial trouble.

Steps to solve its problems began in the usual way, with cutbacks in materials and maintenance. As things got worse, the hospital had to lay off almost 20% of its nonmedical work force, among whom were many loyal, long-term employees. The first results were a plunge in morale and the growth of an underground rumor mill that fueled a growing sense of disaster. Survivors of the "purge" believed that another layoff was imminent. Employee loyalty gave way to resentment that the organization had sold out to "mere" economic forces and had abandoned its moral responsibilities to its employees and patients.

The professional administrators who managed Mercy's business affairs argued for even more cutbacks, particularly in the volume of nonpaying charity care. The nuns, who constituted the hospital's board of directors, refused to turn any charity case away. The chief administrator, caught in the middle of these opposing forces, found that anything he did made someone angry, employees, administrators, or the nuns.

Different visions. Analysis of the situation revealed that part of the problem was that no one had a viable vision of the future. The employees saw the future as a downward path, with slipping standards and fewer people to do what must be done. The nuns saw the future as an extension of the past, taking care of the charity cases and waiting for God to take care of the finances. The administrators saw the future as short and bleak unless something could be done quickly to stop financial losses. The chief administrator, who was not a particularly strong leader, could not mold these dire visions into anything that held promise, and he had no vision of his own to present. As a result, the organization had no sense of direction, except perhaps inextricably toward closing its doors. To an outsider, the organization looked like some large, wounded animal, waiting in stunned confusion for the fatal blow.

Turning point. As things turned out, the nuns may have had the right idea. Sometime earlier, the hospital, as a half-hearted experiment, had opened two satellite clinics in fairly middle-class neighborhoods. Patients from the surrounding neighborhoods used them because they were accessible and convenient. Although the clinics followed the central hospital's policy on charity care, not many charity cases came in, and the clinics quickly became profitable. Although Mercy had not really paid much attention, in other cities clinics like these were proving to be equally successful. They fit well with the industry's increasing emphasis on health maintenance and preventive care while using central hospitals as technical centers to which patients could be sent for more comprehensive care.

Vision building. On the advice of a management consultant, a "vision task force" was formed, composed of nuns, employees, and administrators. Building on the success of the clinics, the task force developed a vision for Mercy that borrowed heavily from successful examples throughout the health care industry.

The vision outlined the hospital's problems and described the desired future, which was survival of the hospital with the ability to continue serving the poor, as well as avoidance of further layoffs. The envisioned future emphasized decentralization, health maintenance, and preventive care. It stressed retention of Mercy's existing culture, insofar as the culture could accept decentralization and the decreased importance of the central hospital relative to the clinics. It retained charity care and high standards while stressing financial viability. When unveiled in a series of meetings with employees and the medical staff, the vision was quickly approved and widely accepted.

The task force members remarked that as the vision developed, it became clear what would have to be done to realize it. That is, the outlines of the plan were dictated by the vision, just as the shape of the vision was dictated by Mercy's environment and its culture. After the vision had been clearly articulated and broadly approved, the task force began formulating plans for achieving it. In this they turned to the clinics, the various units in the hospital, and to influential people throughout the organization. They all were asked to consider the vision and what their units could contribute to attaining it.

Planning process. The preliminary plan that emerged from this beginning stage was much too conservative. People were disinclined to change enough to make the vision attainable. After some intense lobbying by task force members, another attempt was made. Again, it was too conservative. Four iterations later, the plan began to look vaguely promising. At this point, the task force added its own ideas to produce a final plan that asked more of the units than they had volunteered, but not so much that they rebelled. The major changes were slated to take place over a 5-year period, thus reducing the immediate threat to those most affected. Not everyone applauded the final plan, but it was seen as fair and far better than any alternative that could be proposed.

The plan. Briefly, the plan called for the walk-in clinics at the central hospital to be closed and the neighborhood clinics to be expanded and increased in number, largely by moving personnel from the central hospital. One clinic that was expected to lose money was to be placed in the downtown area to serve the very poor. The other clinics were to be spread throughout the city, particularly in cash-producing middle-class areas. Hospital physicians were to be reassigned to the clinics as their primary workplaces, coming to the central hospital to see their more serious patients. Expensive high-tech equipment that duplicated equipment at other hospitals was to be sold, and the neighborhood clinics would be allowed to refer patients to other hospitals, a practice that had been discouraged in the past. In the same vein, narrow specialties were to be phased out and their resources used to strengthen basic medical care. Referral to other hospitals would be made when exotic illnesses were encountered.

The final version of Mercy's new vision and its accompanying plan was accepted because it accommodated the most important parts of everyone's unique vision: The employees got the potential for keeping their jobs and maintaining high standards of care; the nuns got the potential for continuing charity care; and the administrators got the potential for financial soundness.

Of course, the new emphasis on the clinics and the reduced emphasis on the central hospital were threatening to those people who had vested interests in the status quo. A concerted effort, however, by task force members and others who recognized the new vision's potential for saving the organization was effective in converting enough holdouts that the plan finally was accepted and implementation begun. There have been successes and failures, progress and reversals, but the vision is still in place, and the plan is still unfolding. Some of the old wounds have healed, and the organization appears to be moving toward soundness. No more layoffs have been needed, and employees are again building loyalty to the organization. This is not to say that Mercy Hospital's future is safe and secure, but thus far the plan has worked to move the organization toward its vision.

As this example demonstrates, vision is not the same thing as a plan, nor is it mere fantasy. Mercy's vision was made of fairly commonplace stuff, built on its own good fortune in having opened clinics that worked and on copying successful examples in other cities. The vision was not spawned by some great insight on the part of the chief administrator. Indeed, the man was notable for his lack of imagination. Rather, the vision derived from the simple insight that the clinics were the one bright spot in an otherwise dark picture. Even then, the vision and its plan did not spring full-blown as a complete picture. It was crafted piece by piece through hard work and lots of discussion by the task force, and care was taken to make it compatible with what remained of the organization's culture and with the various visions of its members.

Steller Art Frames Revisited

We end this chapter by checking back in on our fictionalized company, Steller Art Frames. The foregoing examples of vision building make it unnecessary to elaborate on how Steller created its vision except to say that it followed the steps discussed above. The one unusual feature was that Steller's assessment committee undertook the vision building task itself while doing the external and internal assessments (usually different committees do the two jobs). They began by informing Steller's staff, and the board, about what they were finding in the course of their assessments, promoting discussion about the company's future. Slowly it became clear that people were agreed that the company had to find a way to transform itself into a global business if it were to survive. This agreement encouraged the committee to look for new markets abroad, to consider ways of expanding its product line—including licensing of its fastener system—while cutting production costs, and to consider how to transform the jobs of the company's existing employees to support the new business model and how to restructure the organization to better support that new model. The vision was itself more complex than this, but this is the essence. The new manager, The Mighty Carson, undertook to build consensus for the new vision. She also used this as an opportunity to help employees understand just how much their work lives were going to change, in anticipation of getting buy-in when the new plan was unveiled.

Summary

To aid in mastery of this material, summarize it for yourself by filling in this topic outline.

Vision: Motivating Change

I. What vision isn't
   A. The vision isn't the mission
   B. The vision isn't a plan
   C. The vision isn't just for threats
   D. The vision isn't necessarily dramatic

II. Elements of vision
   A. Goals
   B. Priorities
   C. Requirements
   D. Implications

III. Sources of vision
   A. Leaders' vision
   B. Member's vision
   C. Consensus

IV. Evolution and revolution revisited
   A. Evolutionary vision
   B. Revolutionary vision

V. Adequacy of the vision

VI. Two examples of vision building
   A. Suburban fire department
   B. Urban hospital

Exercises

1. Return to the current or retired leader you interviewed previously. Try to come up with your own questions about vision, but you could, for example, ask if the organization even has a widely understood and accepted vision. If not, why not? If so, how did it come to exist? Is it evolutionary or revolutionary or a mix? Is it written down? Does it actually guide what people do? How is it conveyed to newcomers to the organization?

2. Pose the same questions to the other people you have interviewed.

3. Write a short essay on the nature and role of vision and add it to your notebook.

Sources and Further Reading

Gardner, H. (1995). *Leading minds: An anatomy of leadership.* New York: Basic Books.

Janis, I. L. (1972). *Victims of groupthink.* Boston: Houghton Mifflin.

Learning International. (1986). *Strategic vision: A new role for corporate leaders.* Stamford, CT: Author.

Milward, H. B., & Laird, W. (1992). Where does policy come from? In B. G. Peters & B. Rockman (Eds.), *The discipline of public administration.* Chatham, NJ: Chatham House.

Nystrom, P. C., & Starbuck, W. H. (1984, Spring). To avoid organizational crises, unlearn. *Organizational Dynamics, 53–65.*

Pruitt, D. G., & Rubin, J. Z. (1986). *Social conflict: Escalation, stalemate and settlement.* New York: Random House.

Shales, T. (1991, May 8). Lack of vision may hurt NBC future, Tartikoff says. *Tucson Citizen.*

Tregoe, B. B., Zimmerman, J. W., Smith, R. A., & Tobia, P. M. (1989). *Vision in action: Putting a winning strategy to work.* New York: Simon & Schuster.

Weatherly, K. A. (1995). *The rapid assessment of organizational culture using the Organizational Culture Survey: Theory research and application.* Unpublished doctoral dissertation, University of Arizona, Tucson.

Four

Plans: Mapping Change

Prime Responsibility #4: Leaders must work with others in the organization to design a plan for moving the organization toward the envisioned future and to promote understanding through out the organization of how the plan will address the goal agenda in pursuit of the vision.

A s we saw in the examples of the fire department and Mercy Hospital in the preceding chapter, it is almost impossible to think about a vision of the future without thinking about plans: what it will take to get there. But, there are plans and there are plans. Some are detailed and rigid, and others are more opportunistic and intuitive. Which is best depends on the organization and the vision.

Who Needs to Plan?

Proponents of what once was called "scientific management" argued that careful planning is a central feature of effective management and that it is only by adhering to the plan that the organization can prosper. The awful specter of "management by crisis" usually is pointed to as the grim alternative to following a well-structured plan, the idea being that without a plan you will be at the whim of every unanticipated event that comes along. Most leaders know that this argument is wrong.

In addition to the fact that the argument contradicts experience, it has other problems. First, it confuses the vision and the plan. The vision gives stability and direction, not the plan. The plan merely is the blueprint for action that derives from practical elaboration of the vision, within the demands and constraints of the internal and external environments. Hence, to operate without a vision may lead to erratic twists and turns in response to events, but if a vision is in place, the absence of a highly detailed plan is, in some cases, not as big a problem as one might think.

Second, in an unpredictable and chaotic environment, adhering to a detailed plan can cause more trouble than not. A plan is like a set of railroad tracks; the organization tends to follow wherever it leads. If the ground shifts under the tracks so that they no longer lead to the desired goals, thundering down the tracks is not going to get you where you want to go.

Third, some organizations need plans more than others. Large organizations need plans in order to coordinate the actions of their many different units; the vision seldom is sufficient for the fine tuning needed to produce this coordination. Without a plan to give some sort of unity to the multiplicity of activities in the different parts of the organization, coordination can be very difficult. In part, this arises because communication is more cumbersome in large organizations than in small ones. Even in this electronic age, it is difficult to quickly inform everyone about what is going on and what needs to be done next. In contrast, because small organizations frequently have an easier job of communicating, they often can coordinate among units without having to spell out everything in advance in a detailed plan.

When he was still an army general, Dwight D. Eisenhower is supposed to have said, "The plan is nothing. Planning is everything." That is, the plan is merely temporary. It must change to fit changing conditions. On the other hand, the thinking and learning that planning requires make flexibility possible when things make the plan obsolete. Having thought through the issues and gathered relevant information, planners are able to understand changes in conditions and adapt their actions to them. Seldom does an organization do exactly what its plan dictates, and seldom does it achieve precisely the vision it started out to achieve. Instead, just as in one's private experience, the organization's vision and its priorities change as the plan is implemented and feedback reveals changes either in the organization or in the environment. The world (and organizations, and people) is a dynamic place, and a plan is of value only if it helps the organization attain desirable results. Otherwise it's an encumbrance and counterproductive, and the organization might well be better off without it.

What's more, even if a plan never needs changes as events unfold, nobody constantly keeps it in mind anyway. When implementing a particular aspect of a plan, attention is on that specific activity and little else. But the vision, which is what gives reason and direction to the plan, must come to mind from time to time to ensure that progress is being made in the right direction or to take into account changes that have come about. The process is like the activity of a long-distance swimmer who has a plan for swimming from one point to another. At any moment, she concentrates on getting the stroke right, on breathing correctly, and on plowing ahead, but every now and then she looks up and makes sure she's still headed in the right direction. Sometimes, perhaps because the current changes or a strong wind blows, she has to adjust her route. Then, having made the change, she goes back to concentrating on the stroke, breathing, and making progress toward her goal.

How to Build a Plan

There are three different levels of plans. A *strategic plan* translates the vision into a set of general long-term goals and the broad thrust of actions that is designed to attain them. An *operating plan* is a portion of the strategic plan that describes concrete, medium-term goals and the concrete actions that are designed to attain them. A *task plan* is a portion of an operating plan that describes highly precise, short-term goals and the specific activities that are designed to attain them. Strategic level goals are designed to address the threats and opportunities in the organization's external and internal environments. Operating level goals are designed to provide changes in the organization's structure and functions that will facilitate attainment of strategic goals and support task level goals. Task level goals are designed to use the changes at the operating level to make changes in specific procedures for producing and distributing products and services that will move the organization toward attainment of its strategic goals. Consider our fictionalized company, Steller Art Frames. Steller's strategic plan was to reduce costs and increase sales. As part of this, two bold moves emerged: One was to move the company to leased quarters in a new enterprise zone to reduce taxes, employing high-turnover young people from the surrounding community to make a new line of frames. The other was to move the production of its mission-style frames to Mexico, employing low-turnover older workers at a wage that was higher than the local norm but lower than similarly skilled workers would have to be paid in the United States. Within this, one of a number of task plans was to set up a program to teach Steller's skilled frame makers how to train enterprise zone and Mexican workers to make quality frames and to direct the administrative staff in selling Steller's present building and arranging the new facilities in both the enterprise zone and Mexico.

Large organizations often have a vision that extends years into the future, and their various plans reflect this time span. Smaller organizations, or organizations in very rapidly changing environments (computer software firms, for example, or disaster relief agencies), operate on much shorter time spans, and their plans reflect these spans. In fact, the strategic plan may not even cover the entire time span of the vision. Knowing that too much can happen to disrupt or antiquate a plan that covers, say, 10 years, the strategic plan may acknowledge a horizon corresponding to the vision's 10-year span but may itself be for only, say, 5 years or less. This works particularly well if the plan is updated each year. The vision keeps things on track, but the shorter time span and frequent revision permits flexibility to deal with unfolding events.

Participation

Before planning proceeds, decisions have to be made about who will oversee creation of the plan and who will contribute to it and how. Usually there is a planning committee, sometimes composed of top leaders and the heads of units within the organization or, in large organizations, a planning staff that does the job on a permanent basis. The point is that there has to be a focal point, a single person or office, to whom information can be forwarded for integration into the plan and who makes sure the planning process proceeds on schedule.

Deciding who participates can be a problem. If the vision and the plan are merely issued by the leadership, they never belong to the rest of the organization, and, perhaps more important, it's possible that the members of the organization may never really understand them. There are various levels of understanding. For example, one can read something and comprehend it well enough to pass an exam but never really understand it in any depth. A plan that comes in a nice folder with lovely diagrams tends to be understood in this superficial way. Real understanding comes from participation—from contributing, from knowing why this was included and that was not, how a subtle point contributes to this or that important goal—and from really *knowing* what the vision and the plan are all about and what the implications are for you and for your coworkers.

Of course, trying to get everyone in the organization around a table for a big discussion probably won't work. Far better is a mixture of top-down, bottom-up vision building and planning. This involves asking the various units in the organization to formulate their own ideas about the vision and then send an informed representative to vision/planning sessions.

Units. After the vision has been articulated and the mission statement drafted, it is time to return to the organization's various units. Their job is to look at their unit's current activities in light of the vision and to decide what must be done to align the two: in short, what the unit must do to contribute to achievement of the vision. Their ideas must be expressed in concrete operational goals and activities, but not necessarily in tactical goals; the tactical level of detail is for use within the unit itself and is often too specific to be of value in the larger plan that is evolving at the organizational level.

A major part of a unit's analysis consists of figuring out where it is now so it can decide how to get where the vision wants it to be. This means that it must gather data about its external and internal environments (Chapter 1). A major function of the planning committee or planning staff is to help procure this information for the units and to supply the units with similar information about the organization as a whole.

Committee. The information from the units is then passed back to the planning committee or planning staff. Their job is to mold the contributions of the various units into an overall plan for the organization. This is a much more difficult job than it seems because each unit's attention is so narrowly directed to its functions and problems that the different pieces do not always fit together well. Sometimes major reformulation is necessary, changing the level of description or even going back to the units and helping them think things through from a different perspective. Through all of this, however, the planning committee must see itself as the facilitator of the process rather than as the primary actor, or the plan that emerges will belong to it rather than to the units and the organization as a whole.

The Focus of Planning

At each level of planning, the unit's, the division's, and the organization's attention is focused on three questions:

- Where are we now?
- Where do we want to be, and when?
- How do we get there from here?

"Where we are now" is determined by Chapter 1's environmental assessment: external opportunities and threats and internal strengths and weaknesses. External opportunities may be new markets or ways of expanding present markets. External threats can include actions by competitors or government regulators or an increasingly soft market for a particular product line. Internal strengths may be such things as the organization's structure or its relations with its members. Internal weaknesses may be such things as underutilized assets or an inflexible and intransigent workforce.

It is important to remember that the external environment consists of both the small part that is of direct interest to the organization (its customers, competitors, or its labor market) and the larger environment that has an indirect, but important, impact (the economy as a whole, free trade agreements with other countries, and the repercussions that quite remote events may have for the organization). It pays to know the competition as well as one knows one's customers (and this is as true for an opera company as it is for a manufacturing company), and it pays to know the national economy as well as one knows the local economy.

"Where we want to be and when" is answered in large part by the vision. But the vision only gives the broad framework; the details are more concrete and take place in real time. Thus it makes sense to translate the goals of the vision into objectives for concrete action at the operational level. For businesses, these objectives are financial, sales, product, human resource, and broader community considerations. For other kinds of organizations, the list will be a little different, but surprisingly similar. Every organization has to pay attention to finances if it is to survive. Every organization has to consider what it is doing and how well that will be accepted by the target population. (If you run a soup kitchen, your customers may not be too particular, but the soup must meet minimal standards or even they will go elsewhere, leaving you with a lot of bad soup and nothing to do.) Every organization has to deal with its members. And every organization has to live in a larger community and maintain some sort of acceptable relations with it.

"How we get there from here" is what most of us think of as the essence of planning. It consists of saying, "We are here, and we want to go there," and "This is the path that connects the two." Of course, there may be different possible paths, and choices must be made among them because not just any path will do. It must not use resources that are urgently needed elsewhere, it must have the potential to reach its objective, and it must be a reasonable and acceptable way of getting there. Most of all, it must be concrete and doable, for this is not the time for empty promises and wild gambles.

John Kotter studied successful general managers (GMs) in nine corporations. One of the things he observed was the following:

> In selecting specific activities to include in their agendas, GMs look for those that accomplish multiple goals, that are consistent with all other goals and plans, and that are within their power to implement. Projects and programs that seem important and logical but do not meet these criteria tend to be discarded or are at least resisted. (Kotter, 1982, p. 161)

Task Definition and Assignment

As planning moves from its initial stages, it is wise to start defining the specific tasks that will be undertaken by specific units of the organization. This serves two purposes: First, if you cannot clearly define the tasks that will move the plan forward, it is likely that the plan is incapable of producing the desired results. It's time to rethink things. Second, task definition allows you to consider to whom responsibility for each task should be assigned.

Definition of tasks links the plan to the real world. Research shows that the biggest difference between successful and unsuccessful implementations of plans is that the unsuccessful ones lack detailed definitions of the component tasks. Thus, if the plan cannot be divided into well-defined tasks, something is wrong with the plan. If the tasks do not look like they can be accomplished within the timelines, something is wrong with the plan. If nobody in the organization is equipped to accomplish the task, something is wrong with the plan. If resources are insufficient to support the task, something is wrong with the plan.

In short, tying the plan to specific, workable tasks often results in the plan being revised and sharpened, in identification of problems that must be solved before the plan can be properly implemented, and in making the plan concrete and clear to everyone involved. Unrealistic goals may be trimmed back, new people with specific skills may be hired, and resources may be shifted from one part of the organization to the other, with the result that the vision and its plan move from being dreams about a desired future to being a set of specific instructions for getting there.

Once task definition is successful, it is time to think about who will have responsibility for each task and how their efforts will contribute to the whole. If a task does not require participation of everyone in the unit, or if the unit has more than one task to accomplish, it is often wise to assign responsibility for each task to a team, with a single team member being designated as the team leader. The team and its leader have the job of making sure that the task gets done within the plan's timelines.

Task Plans

After tasks are defined and assigned to responsible units, teams, and individuals, it is wise to develop specific task plans (also called action plans). Here each step in the task is listed, preferably chronologically. In addition, a date for accomplishment of that step is assigned, and the resources that are necessary for accomplishing it are listed. An individual is assigned responsibility for the task as a whole, and he or she uses the task plan as a guide for seeing that the various steps are accomplished in a timely manner. If steps must be accomplished simultaneously, or if some steps depend on other steps having been accomplished previously, it often is helpful to design a chart that displays progress on each task as a function of time. There are standard ways of designing such charts that can be adopted for the task at hand.

The Monitor

Assigning tasks to units, teams, and individuals; breaking the tasks into steps; and providing resources for accomplishing the parts is not the whole story. Clearly, what has been done in this process is to distribute the responsibility for accomplishment of the various aspects of the plan throughout the organization, assigning responsibility for implementation to appropriate groups and individuals. But someone has to oversee these distributed activities to make sure that everything throughout the organization is coming together properly.

Oversight requires gathering of information about progress on the tasks from each group and concentrating that information at one point so that someone, a *monitor,* can get a picture of progress for the plan as a whole. The monitor may be a group or an individual: the planning committee, the executive committee, the leader of the organization, or a specially appointed person such as a vice president for planning.

Measurement

Whatever the organization's objectives, a major part of the planning process consists of incorporating ways to measure progress toward them. This can be difficult for "soft" objectives like community relations; merely counting the number of "hate letters" per month is probably not adequate. A decrease in such letters could mean that relations are improving, or it could mean that letter writers have given up and are plotting with their lawyers for something more forceful. Quite often, the effort to design ways of measuring progress toward objectives produces a side benefit. Thinking about measurement focuses attention on what constitutes progress, and this leads to consideration of the actions that will in fact bring progress about. The result is that the activities that are proposed as part of the operational plan become clearer and more narrowly directed toward accomplishment of the objectives. In addition, analyzing the activities permits various stages in them to be designated as *milestones* that can be used to identify progress on the path toward the goals.

Timelines

Activities aimed at achievement of objectives must unfold in time, and all of the various elements (including materials and tools and people) must be properly coordinated in time or even the best plan will end in shambles. Therefore, operating and task plans should be structured along a timeline and their milestones assigned specific times for accomplishment. Moreover, use of this common time structure for different units allows the planning committee to use time as an overall framework when it starts to mold the various units' task plans *and* the resulting operating plans into a strategic plan. If things do not come together in time, if they do not all fit within the planning horizon and ultimately within the horizon of the vision, the organization simply will not operate as a coordinated entity.

Communicating the Vision and Plan

When the vision springs from the existing culture and ongoing activities, or when the need for change and the nature of that change is obvious to most members of the organization, your job is relatively easy. Because the vision permeates the organization, your task is simply to clarify it, to make it crisp and add details. This doesn't mean that achieving the vision is going to be easy. Rather, it means that the work can begin without first building consensus behind the proposals. The problems that the vision addresses may be thorny and the dangers they present may be daunting, but the presence of a consensus makes the task comparatively easy. But when consensus does not exist naturally, your first priority is to build it.

Rules of Communication

There are six rules for effectively communicating the vision and the plan, and of building consensus about them:

1. Use concrete language that outlines the goals and the sequence of things that must be done.

2. Check to make sure people, in fact, understand the vision and its plan.

3. Maintain your own, the vision's, and the plan's credibility.

4. Insofar as possible, only ask for small steps toward change, allowing people to adjust in stages. If this is not possible, then explain why not and clearly explain what the big step will involve.

5. Underscore the vision's reasonableness and the plan's potential for success.

6. Repeat the explanation of the vision and the plan whenever the opportunity arises.

(Adapted from Tregoe, Zimmerman, Smith, & Tobia, 1989)

The first rule, *concreteness*, simply says that to be communicated successfully, both the vision and its plan must be presented in simple, specific terms. For most people, this means that the vision must have no more than two or three broad, well-defined, superordinate goals; more than this makes the vision too complicated to understand or remember. The plan must contain the sequence of steps required to realize the vision, thus precisely defining the goals and demonstrating that they are reachable. This action orientation gives everyone a common framework for talking and thinking about the vision and its plan.

The second rule, *understanding*, provides feedback about whether communication has been successful. The simplest test is whether activity starts to change in ways that conform to the plan and promote the vision. More complicated tests may involve asking people to tell you what they think the new vision is and to describe the plan for getting there. A particularly valuable test is to ask for outlines of how the new vision and plan will affect the person's own unit and his or her own job. And, as was the case when trying to change culture, key opinion makers who accept the new vision and its plan should be encouraged to try to convince others, to make public statements testifying to their acceptance, and in whatever way possible, to make it clear to others (and to themselves) that they are committed.

The third rule, *credibility*, makes it clear that the vision and plan are to be taken seriously. For example, if the vision requires austerity, *everyone* must be affected. Management, supervisors, and employees, and most of all, *you* must work harder, do without customary perks, take pay cuts, and so on. This is particularly important if some units are affected more than others (spreading some of the misery, even if it's really not wholly necessary for every unit, is a way of showing that "we're all in this together.") A specific example of the importance of credibility occurred a few years ago when British coal miners went on strike, thus forcing a cut in the production of electric power. The cabinet minister in charge outlined a vision in which austerity would allow everyone to have enough electricity to get by and the economy would not be too adversely affected by shortages. His plan called for everyone to conserve electricity by turning off everything that could be turned off. The country accepted his vision and followed his plan, even though it was winter and most homes were heated by electricity. In fact, some people were so steadfast in following the plan that they became quite ill because they refused to turn on the heat. Then a national newspaper featured a picture of the cabinet minister's London townhouse ablaze with lights. As his credibility fell and his plan disintegrated, the use of electricity quickly increased.

The fourth rule, *small steps when possible*, which is related to evolutionary change, means that the vision must not be radical and must not grossly violate the current culture or it will be rejected out of hand. The best policy is to outline present problems, which will often be broadly recognized already. Then, looming threats or opportunities must be explained. The general outline of the new vision and its plan can then be presented, with an explanation of how they address the problems, threats, and opportunities and, equally important, with an explanation of how they derive from and preserve the most sacred beliefs in the current culture. As acceptance of this reasoning grows, the details of the new vision and its plan can be filled in at appropriate times. The key is to build consensus incrementally, building on acceptance and keeping within the broad outline that was presented originally. Every attempt must be made to remain above board and to provide both the appearance and substance of honesty and openness about what is taking place.

Of course, as with evolutionary change, incrementally communicating the vision and plan may be inappropriate if the organization is in such peril that everyone knows that something radical must be done or it will die. Extreme danger calls for extreme action, and a revolutionary vision may be greeted with relief. Even here, however, the new vision cannot ignore the existing culture. It cannot solve the organization's problems by completely selling out everything the organization stands for. Bold new ideas may inspire people, but close inspection usually shows that they are not bold because they destroy the organization's beliefs and values. Rather, they are bold because they address the problem in a way that has not been done before while preserving those beliefs and values.

The fifth rule, *reasonableness,* means that not only must the new vision be shown to relate to the organization's culture; it also must be shown to be sound. In part, this means showing that the vision holds the key to a desirable future and that its plan offers the possibility of solving immediate problems or coping with threats and opportunities confronting the organization. And, in part, it means demonstrating that the vision and plan were arrived at by a reasonable process by knowledgeable people. And, finally, it means that it is possible to imagine actually achieving success.

When people fear for the future, they often get caught up in the rhetoric of a new vision and allow themselves to be convinced that it offers the only hope. Most people also possess fairly reliable nonsense detectors, however, and in the cold light of day they can tell if what is being proposed has substance. If it looks to them as though there is a strong likelihood of failure, they will resist. Similarly, even a promising vision and plan that appear to have been arrived at arbitrarily will be resisted. And, if the implications for their own roles in the organization are not made clear, most people will regard the proposals as risky and resist them. That is, members have to know how what they do fits into the vision and how changing what they do to accommodate the plan will contribute to the organization's success.

The sixth rule, *repetition*, makes sure the members do not lose track of where things are going and why. Explaining the vision and its plan once is not enough. As one executive told me, "I can't assume that my people understand the vision for this company, and even when they do, they seem to forget it. A large part of my job is repeating, over and over again, what it is we are trying to do and why we are trying to do it."

Because it summarizes the vision and focuses on activities, the mission statement is one way of conveying the vision repeatedly. To be effective, the mission statement must be part of nearly everything: framed above each desk, on posters beside the elevators, printed on the stationery, and included as a preface to reports and publications. One company has its mission statement printed on T-shirts so it will be with employees during their time off. Another hands out small plastic cards with a calendar on one side and the mission statement on the other. Employees carry them in their wallets and purses or use them as bookmarks. More than one company has its mission statement hung on the wall of the foyer so everyone sees it on the way to work in the morning.

By the same token, the plan must be repeated lest people forget about it. The fact is that most plans end up carefully filed away, never to be seen again. Leadership at all levels must make sure that the plan becomes an integral part of everyday life. Copies of the relevant parts should be kept at hand. It should be reviewed before meetings so that decisions take it into account. Members of the organization should be able to describe it, and their actions should reflect it. And all of this only happens if leaders do it themselves. It does no good to tell others to heed the plan if it is clear that leadership has no intention of doing so. If the plan is worth formulating, it ought to be worth repeating, and it ought to be worth following. Flexibility is necessary, of course, but the plan is there to ensure that everyone is working toward the same goals. Without it, things quickly revert to the conditions that prompted its formulation in the first place.

Providing Resources

Flexibility and persistence provide the attitudinal foundations for implementation. They cannot, however, do the job alone. One must plan for implementing the plan. That is, one must anticipate what will be required to implement the plan and provide those resources in a timely manner.

The major resources are time, money, organizational structure, people, and a code of conduct.

Time

Allowing adequate time to get things done and providing time for unexpected delays are central to success. After having invested in vision building and planning, however, both of which take time, leaders often become bored with the process and want to move on to new challenges. As a result they tend to underestimate the time that implementation will require, and by restricting the schedule, they condemn the plan to trouble, if not to failure.

In the mid-1980s, a survey was conducted of 93 private sector firms, coupled with interviews with the CEOs of 21 of the firms and 25 heads of governmental agencies (Alexander, 1985). They were asked about the problems that they had encountered in the course of implementing plans within their respective organizations. The most frequently cited problem was that insufficient time had been allocated to do what had to be done. The data showed that even implementations that subsequently succeeded were hampered by the unrealistically short timelines provided for in the plan.

Money

It is no surprise that failure to provide money for implementation can doom a plan. What is less clear, however, is how money is to be provided. Other than the obvious question of where it is to come from, there is the question of how it is to be delivered. That is, there can be an amount set aside to be used as it is needed, which prevents its use elsewhere in the meantime. Or, it can be provided as it is needed for the implementation. This runs the danger of getting caught up in the "sunk costs" trap: each increment in funding is so small relative to what already has been spent that it seems a shame not to spend it in the hope of salvaging the whole amount through success. If progress is being made, this may be a reasonable way to think. But, if even more money is spent in the hope of salvaging a failing plan, this action introduces more risk. If one is not careful, the bill grows far greater, far faster than anyone realizes, and it all may be for naught.

Money plays a central role in implementation in the form of incentives and rewards. It is surprising how many organizations use performance evaluation and compensation systems that work against implementation rather than for it. Evaluation and compensation are both valuable in themselves, but they also are a form of feedback to group members about what kinds of actions are required of them. If the system fails to reward actions that are necessary for success, people are less likely to do them. The sad fact is that many evaluation and compensation systems actually penalize the actions they want to promote, often emphasizing short-term performance, neglecting the long-term performance that is necessary for implementation of any but the simplest plans. This is particularly damaging in the early stages of implementation when group members are switching from old activities to new ones as they begin implementation of the new plan. Transition usually results in some confusion and a drop in productivity until new routines are established and the requirements of the new plan become clear. One can hardly blame people for going slowly if they know that any error will result in penalty. Even later in implementation, it may be necessary to take temporary losses in order to make long-term gains. People must not be penalized for those losses, or they will strive to avoid them, thus forfeiting the long-term gains required for the plan's success and the vision's realization.

Organizational Structure

If the organization lacks the mechanisms or channels for implementing parts of the plan, implementation either will stop or will be badly slowed while people improvise. A symphony orchestra is unlikely to succeed at fund raising if everything is left up to the orchestra members. Even the best musician may know nothing about designing brochures, planning mailings, setting up accounting systems for the donations, and all the rest. Before beginning such a venture, the orchestra must modify its structure to provide the functions that are required. For arts organizations, this often involves formation of foundations ("Friends of the Symphony"), leaving the details to a few paid managers and a brigade of talented volunteers. Alternatively, it may hire a commercial fund-raising organization.

Similarly, if a manufacturing firm's vision calls for moving into new product areas, provision must be made for designing those new products. It is not sufficient to tell the engineering department to spend part of its time inventing. They probably lack the skills, and they already have jobs to do. If the firm does not want to have the design done by outsiders, it must change its structure to include a design unit and then must staff that unit.

Structure and history. Organizations' structures reflect their history. Most areas of endeavor (commercial, public, or private) have a typical organizational structure. If the orchestra creates a foundation, it is likely that the foundation will look a great deal like other orchestras' foundations. Heavy manufacturing companies tend to look alike; grocery stores have similar structures; and so on. In large part this makes sense, but when organizations start to change, to become something different from what they were, they often fail to modify their structures adequately. This results in difficulties because although the old structure may well have been well suited to the old enterprise, it very well may be wrong for the new one.

Communications. One of the first casualties of inappropriate structure is communication. It is difficult enough to communicate within an organization, but unit boundaries often are virtually impenetrable. Organizations often tack new units onto the existing structure and, in so doing, grow in truly bizarre ways. When the organization needs to change, established patterns of communication among the units may become outmoded, but it is difficult to establish new ones. Sometimes revolutionary restructuring is required, but even then, the residuals of the old structure may haunt the organization.

Structure as a tool. An organization's structure is not a convenience; it is the core of how things get done. It is analogous to a tool that is specially designed to do a particular task. It can be used for some other task, but not efficiently and often not effectively. Unfortunately, resistance to restructuring is usually even greater than resistance to a new vision or plan. The culture and the structure are closely interwoven; friendships are dictated by structure; familiar work routines rely on structure; and even the location at which particular jobs are done depends on structure. As one would expect, the degree of resistance that is generated by proposed changes in structure depends on the organization members' commitment to the vision and plan that necessitate those changes. This is another reason why it is so important to bring the members on board in regard to the vision and the plan. If there is consensus and commitment, members will be less inclined to revolt when structural changes are required.

People

Executives often say that people are the organization's most important resource, a cliché, but an accurate cliché. Implementation affects the members of the organization in two major ways. The first impact is a need for communication about the implementation: communication *to* them about what is expected of them (and why) and communication *from* them about the success of their efforts, the barriers they have encountered, and the surprises they have experienced. The second impact is a need for help in coping with changes that come about both in aid of implementation and as a result of implementation. Whether the plan succeeds or fails, their lives will be affected, often radically. They will need to learn new skills on the job or through training. They will need to work compatibly with new people, either people from other parts of the organization or people hired as a result of the implementation. They may well need to work in a new location, either somewhere nearby or perhaps on the other side of the continent or in another country.

Organizations that think of their employees as so many hired energy units usually fail to plan ways to ease the impacts of implementation, unless it will save financial resources. Historically, the result has been an understandable cynicism on the part of employees, a lack of loyalty, and a lack of trust. The financial loss resulting from this hostility is incalculable.

Organizations that take a more enlightened view—usually organizations that require technically trained people or have difficulty recruiting and retaining members—find that they profit in the long run by planning ways to ease the impacts of implementation on members. In some cases, not all that much is required; if people know what to expect and have time to digest it, they usually can adjust. No one wants to sell a house, leave friends, and move to a new town. But, given time to think about it, time to adjust to the idea, many find it's not as awful as it at first sounds. So, too, no one wants to have to take a difficult training course in computers, but on reflection it might seem like just the right thing to enliven a stale, boring job. People are wonderfully resilient, but they need to see what's coming and have time to adjust. They're right when they think the organization owes them the courtesy of keeping them informed of what's going to happen to them.

Code of Conduct

Prior to, or concurrent with, the plan being constructed, work must be devoted to writing a code of conduct so people will know what is expected of them as they go about the organization's business. It is, of course, far too late to teach them morals, something they supposedly learned at their mother's knee. And nobody likes to think they have to be instructed in ethics. But most people understand that the unique nature of the activities required by any particular organization gives rise to uniquely dangerous situations, and they are open to instruction about how to deal with those situations. An organization that does not have a formal, written code of conduct is leaving itself open to each individual member's interpretation of what constitutes dangerous situations and his or her personal assessment of what to do in such situations. The code gives uniformity to both detection of danger and dealing with it by providing a set of rules, reinforced by clearly delineated penalties for violating those rules.

A code of conduct is broader than morals and ethics. It includes legal issues, and it sets the general tone for how the organization's members should interact with each other and with outsiders. Dangerous situations are of two kinds: those in which inappropriate conduct can result in unwarranted personal gains and those in which inappropriate conduct can result in unwarranted gains to the organization. Examples of unwarranted personal gains are abuse of power (as in sexual harassment), abuse of knowledge (as in insider trading), abuse of access (as in misappropriation of the organization's physical or intellectual property), and abuse of affiliation (as in using membership to suggest the organization endorses one's own political or social agenda). Examples of unwarranted organizational gain are abuse of power (as in intimidation or bribery of public officials at home or abroad), abuse of knowledge (as in intentional misrepresentation of the organization's financial status to investors or lenders), abuse of access (as in unfairly obtaining information about competing bids in order to underbid them), and abuse of affiliation (as in colluding with similar organizations to fix prices or prevent access to markets). A code of conduct is central to efforts to change an organization's culture, even if the old culture already supports ethical conduct. This is because it provides a very clear statement of what is expected as the organization changes and unfamiliar, dangerous situations arise.

In the drive to make implementation successful, it is easy for the organization's members to get the impression that any and all means are acceptable as long as they produce results. An explicit code of conduct, stated as organizational policy, helps to counter this impression.

The best way to construct a code of conduct is to convene a group composed of a cross section of the organization (election of members by the various constituencies can work). The goal is to avoid the appearance of the code being imposed from the top, as well as make sure that it addresses the dangerous situations encountered across the entire organization.

The code-writing committee should begin by reviewing examples of existing codes, both for this organization (if it already has one) and for other organizations. The Center for the Study of Ethics in the Professions at the Illinois Institute of Technology has compiled a large collection of codes that is available on the Internet (http://ethics.iit.edu/codes/index .html). This site also has links to helpful articles about how to write a code (By the way, IBM's code is a particularly instructive example).

As with any policy document, a code of conduct is useless if people do not read it or if they believe that ignoring it will have no real consequences. This means that it has to be properly disseminated and a mechanism must be provided to make sure it is read and properly understood (perhaps an examination on its contents). People hate to read these sorts of things because they already believe themselves to be ethical and because the dangerous situations do not look all that dangerous in the abstract. Clearly delineated, severe consequences of violating the code improve motivation to read it.

As one of the characters said about sins in the TV movie *The Flame Trees of Thika* (1982), "When other people commit them [sins] it's shocking. When you do it, it seems quite natural" (which, of course, is the great problem about behaving ethically). Even if one is a paragon of integrity, dangerous situations seldom come with bright red labels. When the full flush of possible success is upon us, wisdom may counsel prudence and principle, but the excitement of the moment may push us forward anyway. The purpose of a code of conduct is to inoculate us, as much as possible, by encoding ethics as a list of explicit rules that stand as organizational policy for dealing with dangerous situations. Thus, it must be made clear to everybody (including you) that even if a particular behavior might not violate their personal ethics, the organization's policy takes precedence when they are engaged in the organization's business.

Steller Again

To close this chapter, let us return to Steller Art Frames. Recall that Poor Wayne's replacement, The Mighty Carson, had set up an assessment committee that evolved into the vision committee and then became the planning committee. When we last visited them, they were considering a move to leased space in an enterprise zone and setting up facilities in Mexico, turning Steller's highly skilled shop supervisors into full-time trainers, hiring new workforces in the zone and in Mexico, and training the Mexican workers to make mission-style frames and the zone workers to make a new line of frames, thereby expanding Steller's product offerings and, hopefully, increasing sales. All of this became more feasible after the assessment process made five discoveries, all of which presented the company with opportunities.

The first discovery was mentioned before: Steller's patented fastener system was equally useful for furniture joints. With appropriate steps to protect the patent rights, Steller had the opportunity to license the system in the furniture industry.

The second discovery was that a large corporation wanted to buy a building in the city's revitalized historic district for conversion to a restaurant, and Steller's building was precisely what they wanted. Sale of the building was an opportunity to obtain cash that would help Steller through its transition. Moreover, the lease terms for space in a city-owned warehouse in the enterprise zone turned out to be very favorable, including help with remodeling costs.

The third discovery was the little-known fact that many Germans were raised on adventure stories about cowboys and the old West and retained an insatiable fascination with the American West, including mission-style furniture and interior decor.[1] Moreover, the German fascination appears to be contagious because it has spread to Austria, the Scandinavian countries, and eastern Europe. By establishing ties with the major European distributor of Western art and mission-style furniture, Steller had the opportunity to establish itself as the premier product line in Germany, Austria, Scandinavia, and eastern Europe, a huge market that none of Steller's competitors had discovered.

The fourth discovery was that the publicity surrounding a major exhibit of art deco crafts and furniture at the Boston Museum of Fine Arts (then moving to other museums throughout the country) caused a resurgence of interest in both art deco and art nouveau furniture and accessories. Jimmy, a frame maker who was taking design courses in night school, pointed out that many of Steller's mission-style designs could be modified to become deco and nouveau designs, allowing Steller the opportunity to enter this potentially lucrative new market quickly and with little change in its production methods.

Without going into details, the plan that the committee proposed followed from the information given above. Then the committee sat down with Carson to discuss how the company would provide resources for implementation. The first problem was money to see Steller through the transition, which would occur in two stages. First, the Mexican facility would be established to provide a continuous flow of mission-style frames during implementation of the second stage: moving to the enterprise zone and beginning production of a new line of art deco and art nouveau frames. Carson took responsibility for raising money by selling Steller's building and borrowing the remainder. In addition, the committee and Carson agreed on a ballpark amount that could be spent on implementing the new plan, beyond which there would be an automatic review of the whole thing to make sure they weren't simply throwing good money after bad.

The second problem was the proposed timelines. Carson was afraid the board of directors would want things to move considerably more quickly for fear the company would fail before the plan could be implemented and the company's fortunes turned around. After working out the details of what was involved in each segment of the plan, however, she was prepared to defend the timelines to the board with the support of its ex officio representative on the committee.

Carson quickly agreed to the committee's recommendations for pay raises for the new trainers (the former supervisors) and for paying a consultant to teach them to be more professional at it. Provision was made for three experienced frame makers, who were poised for promotions, to move to Mexico to be production supervisors in the new facility, with appropriate raises.

The committee recommended that the old, rather haphazard structure of the organization be abandoned and a new, explicit, divisional structure be adopted to support the new way the organization was going to work. There would be a training division, a division located in Mexico for mission-style frames, a division located in the enterprise zone for art deco and art nouveau frames, a domestic sales division, a European sales division, and an administrative support division (for inventory management, procurement, billing, shipping, accounting, etc). In addition, a division would be established to deal with licensing of Steller's patented fastener system and another division created for marketing and in-house catalogue production, given that one catalogue (both mission-style and deco/nouveau frames) would be produced in English for the United States, a similar one in English and French for Canada, and another (mission style) in a variety of languages for Europe.

As a prelude to unveiling the plan, Carson agreed to undertake face-to-face discussions with the board and with employees to keep them up to date on what was going on so nobody would be surprised when the first draft of the plan was distributed. Their suggestions would be fed back to the committee, and they would be asked to comment on the draft of the plan before it was finalized.

Finally, Carson agreed to set up a new committee to design a code of conduct that would be compatible with the new structure and goals of the company. This was deemed especially important because the company was going to grow larger and would have sites in both Mexico and the United States. The fear was that growth and geographical division would make it more difficult to monitor the conduct of employees and that guidelines were necessary to ensure that everyone knew how to behave when they were acting on behalf of the company. The committee also recommended that a draft of the code of conduct be submitted to everyone in the organization for comment before it was finalized. Finally, they recommended that part of the training program for new employees include intensive study of the code of conduct.

Having decided all of this, Carson and the committee were ready to turn to finalization of the plan and to undertaking its implementation. An implementation committee was appointed to take over from the planning committee; most members were volunteers, and Carson appointed herself the chair so she would be very visible as the leader of the effort.

Summary

To aid in the mastery of this material, summarize it for yourself by filling in this topic outline.

Plans: Mapping Change

I. Who needs to plan?

II. How to build a plan
   A. Participation
      1. Units
      2. Committee

III. The focus of planning

IV. Task definition and assignment
   A. Task plans
   B. The monitor
   C. Measurement
   D. Timelines

V. Communicating the vision and plan
   A. Rules of communication

VI. Providing resources
   A. Time
   B. Money
   C. Organizational structure
      1. Structure and history
      2. Communications
      3. Structure as a tool
   D. People
   E. Code of conduct

Note

1. Although most Americans have never heard of him, Karl May (1842–1912) is the most popular German author, ever. He wrote 60 adventure stories about the American West, although it was not until 1908 that he visited the United Sates and even then was never farther west than Buffalo, NY. His books have been translated into 30 languages, have sold over 100 million copies worldwide, and have been the basis of countless movies. Most German males read his books as children, retaining a deep, almost nostalgic, affection for May's fictional West. His work was admired by Albert Einstein, Albert Schweitzer, and Herman Hesse, as well as Adolph Hitler.

Exercises

1. Return to the current or retired leader you have been interviewing and ask about how planning is done in his or her organization. Are there specific people whose job it is to formulate plans? Do they do so for the organization as a whole? For units? Ask to see copies of written documents such as the final plan or plans for units. Ask the leader his or her opinion about the pros and cons of planning and the value of the plan to the organization.

2. Return to your other interviewees and obtain their views about planning. How do their units contribute to the planning process, if they do? Do they have plans specific to their units, and if so, how are these plans derived? How do these plans dovetail with the overall plan? Ask them their opinions about the pros and cons of planning and the value to their units and the organization as a whole.

3. Write an essay incorporating what you have learned about planning and add it to your notebook.

Sources and Further Reading

Alexander, L. D. (1985). Successfully implementing strategic decisions. *Long Range Planning, 18,* 91–97.

Birnbaum, W. S. (1990). *If your strategy is so terrific, how come it doesn't work?* New York: Amacom.

Fisher, R., & Ury, W. (1983). *Getting to yes.* New York: Penguin.

Gordon, G. G. (1991). Industry determinants of organizational culture. *Academy of Management Review, 2,* 396–415.

Hall, W. (1980, September-October). Survival strategies in a hostile environment. *Harvard Business Review,* 75–85.

Hawkesworth, J. (1982, January 17). *The Flame Trees of Thika* [Television series, episode 3 of 7], *Masterpiece Theatre.* New York: Public Broadcasting Service.

Kotter, J. P. (1982, November/December). What effective managers really do. *Harvard Business Review,* 106–114.

Kotter, J. P., & Schlessinger, L. A. (1979, March-April). Choosing strategies for change. *Harvard Business Review,* 106–114.

Mintzberg, H. (1978). Patterns in strategy formation. *Management Science, 24,* 934–948.

Mintzberg, H., & Quinn, J. B. (1991). *The strategy process.* Englewood Cliffs, NJ: Prentice Hall.

Tregoe, B. B., Zimmerman, J. W., Smith, R. A., & Tobia, P. M. (1989). *Vision in action: Putting a winning strategy to work.* New York: Simon & Schuster.

Five

Implementation: Producing Change

*Prime Responsibility #5: Leaders must work with
others to maintain momentum during plan implementation and
to monitor progress in order to discover and correct weaknesses in the plan.*

Having formulated a plan, it's time to implement it. You might think that, as leader of the organization, implementation would be your biggest and most challenging job. You'd be wrong.

The Great Irony of leadership is that during the time that change actually is being implemented, you, the leader, have to step back and leave it to everyone else. If the plan was properly done, they'll know what to do.

Like so many leaders, you probably will find that stepping back isn't easy. But the reasons for doing so are compelling: You can't allow yourself to get caught up in the details of implementation because you have to keep the big picture in mind. You can't get involved in the details because you'll be tempted to get your fingers into everything, particularly when something appears to be going wrong. Everyone has enough to do without having to deal with your meddling.

You won't be idle. You'll have two huge jobs to do to make implementation work. First, you have to act as cheerleader. Second, you have to oversee efforts to monitor the progress of the implementation and, when progress is lacking, work with others to get things back on track.

Cheerleading

Cheerleading is perhaps too whimsical a word for what is, after all, a very important job; you're free to choose something more dignified. Whatever it's called, the point is that you, as leader, have to continually rally everyone to the cause so that momentum isn't lost as the hard work of implementation proceeds. People are going to get tired, be stressed by change, and lose track of the big picture. It's your job to keep reminding them. They'll see the required changes in their jobs as trivial, unreasonable, or even silly, forgetting that implementation consists of countless little changes that add up to big changes. It's your job to keep reminding them. They'll be unable to see overall progress because their portion is so small. It's your job to keep reminding them. In every case, your reminders must help them understand that every little detail of what they're doing is important to making implementation a success.

Cheerleading is a tough job. It begins early on to prepare everyone for the eventuality of change, continues as the plan is introduced, and intensifies as implementation unfolds. It takes enormous amounts of time: You spend your days talking, talking, talking. You have to carry the message to every part of the organization, as well as to the organization's external constituencies. You put in long days, eat lots of tepid chicken dinners, and grow weary of your own voice as you give speech after speech urging people on. You're always the key spokesperson for your organization, but cheerleading is even more intense. People must be kept abreast of what is going on throughout the organization during this stressful time as experiments are attempted and new systems and procedures are installed and tested, as old jobs wither in importance and new ones come into being, and as people get moved around in the organization and have to adjust to new coworkers and responsibilities. Yours must be the calming voice of reason, reassuring everyone that all the work and seeming chaos are worthwhile, that you're on top of things and confident of success.

Cheerleading should be done with an eye to the future. Aside from informing, motivating, and reassuring people, cheerleading establishes the foundation for subsequent institutionalization of the changes that are being made. As we will see in Chapter 6, institutionalization means making sure that the changes in structure, procedures, and culture that are made during implementation endure until they need to be changed again. By stressing successes during implementation, cheerleading puts the best possible light on the changes that brought them about, thus legitimizing them and beginning their integration into the new "normal" for the organization.

Monitoring

You cannot cheerlead convincingly if you have no facts; you must be right about the pace of progress, about successes, and about setbacks. To be right, you must have accurate and timely updates about what is going on. The necessary information is obtained by orderly monitoring of implementation. Even more important than ensuring accurate cheerleading, monitoring serves to tell you where the plan is flawed, allowing for corrective action.

Just as you have no role in the minute details of implementation, you have no role in the minute details of monitoring. Your job as leader is to oversee both of them. Someone with experience in gathering and analyzing data should be appointed as monitor and given staff support. The monitor's job is to organize information as it comes in from functional managers, supervisors, and support staff throughout the organization. Then the monitor (with his or her helpers) digests the information and provides periodic summaries to you and the members of your leadership team, as well as to the implementation committee.

There are three reasons why you should delegate monitoring to someone else. First, you probably don't have the training to do it. Second, you certainly won't have the time to do it if you meet your cheerleading responsibilities. Third, even though variance in data is to be expected, you're likely to react to each random rise or fall as though it were truth itself. The resulting emotional swings will interfere with everything else you have to do. Avoid this wear and tear on yourself, and on those around you, by turning monitoring over to someone else.

What Is Monitored?

One might think that implementation progress should be monitored by measuring how well the organization is coming to cope with the threats and opportunities in its external and internal environments. We will call this *strategic monitoring*. The problem is that results at this level are unlikely to occur very quickly and may not occur at all until implemented changes have been completed and had time to have an effect. Ultimately, of course, this is the measure of the success of the entire change initiative.

In the short run, monitoring focuses on how well implementation itself is progressing, the timeliness of change completion, and the way in which those changes intermesh to create the new ways of doing things prescribed by the plan. We will call this *implementation monitoring*. If the changes interfere with each other, produce unwanted outcomes, or simply do not work, remedies must be applied. Of course, problems will arise simply because everything is new and things will iron themselves out over time. But some problems are signals that things are not going well. Monitoring serves to identify both kinds of problems, but it focuses on those that are real and likely to persist if they are not addressed.

Implementation Monitoring

Implementation monitoring is the general name for evaluation of implementation progress by managers and supervisors throughout the organization, communication of their evaluations to the monitor, and the process of compiling the information and issuing reports to the organization's leaders and the planning group.

The best way to help managers and supervisors do their task is to make them partners in the implementation. This sometimes is done by forming teams at the managerial and the supervisory levels of the organization and making these teams the focal point of implementation monitoring. The number of teams at each level depends on the size and structure of the organization. The purpose of the teams is to support their members (the managers or supervisors) as they make their evaluations and reports. The teams also facilitate communication between the front line, where implementation actually is occurring, and the monitor, and, subsequently, with you and your leadership team.

Supervisors have far more complicated responsibilities than is generally appreciated. Bissell (1992) has dissected their jobs into administrator (reporting, record keeping, oversight, supplies, scheduling, dissemination of changes in policy and procedures), teacher (teaching skills and assessing improvement), parent (modeling work values and attitudes, disciplining, encouraging, protecting, and supporting), counselor (listening, resolving conflicts), and peer (socializing, friendliness). Midlevel managers also have

complex jobs: liaison with upper management, conduits for and dissemi-
nators of information, and spokespeople for their units. On top of all of
this, implementation requires both supervisors and managers to become
part of the monitoring process. The teams are meant to help them with this
new duty and to reduce the added load by allowing them to share insights
about how to go about performing it.

Recall that construction of the plan involved people from every level
of the organization. In addition to encouraging buy-in, involvement provides everyone with at least a general idea about the changes that the plan
requires in their jobs and the jobs of those who report to them. A general
idea is insufficient, however, when it comes time to implement change
and monitor progress. Both require more specificity than usually exists in
the plan. This is where the implementation teams come in: They can help
each supervisor or each manager create a framework for evaluation of
implementation progress in their respective units. By asking questions
and helping individual supervisors or managers clarify their answers to
those questions, they can help create the framework:

1. What are the specific changes that are required?

2. What is the timeline for executing the changes?

3. How do you decide when timelines have slipped so much that implementation is compromised?

4. What are the indicators of success or failure of an implemented change?

5. How do you compare obtained outcomes with those indicators?

6. How much misalignment between indicators and outcomes is allowed
   before a change is regarded as failing?

7. How do you decide whether failure is due to the change or to the people
   who are charged with implementing the change?

8. If failure is a people problem, what do you do?

9. If failure is due to a flaw in the change itself, are there backup plans for
   dealing with it? If not, can remedies be instigated on the local level, or
   must they come from higher in the organization?

10. What do you include in reports to the monitor, and what do you exclude?

The answers to these questions will be unique for each supervisor and
each manager, but if everyone on the team is helping everyone else

address them, there will be a fair amount of uniformity in how they approach monitoring. Of course, the final say is up to the monitor because he or she knows what kind of information is needed to create an overall picture of implementation progress.

We have been talking about change in the broadest possible terms, "generic" change. In reality, of course, change is very specific and highly unique to the individual and unit. Recall from Chapter 4 that the overall plan contains three different levels: strategic, operating, and task. Monitoring corresponds to these levels: Strategic monitoring corresponds to the strategic level and is the responsibility of top management and the organization's leadership. Implementation monitoring corresponds to the operating level and task levels, with middle management responsible for the operating level and supervisors responsible for the task level. For example, part of the strategic level plan may call for increasing sales of add-on products and provision of custom designs for existing customers in order to reduce their defection to competitors. To make this happen, the operating level plan would specify required changes in resource allocations, organizational structure, products, marketing, distribution, sales, communications channels, and the like. The task level plan would specify what is required to make the operating level plan work: staffing, job design, and task procedures. The task level is where the rubber meets the road, where the small changes that add up to the big changes are made to happen, and where their effectiveness must be closely watched. This is the domain of supervisors and the frontline employees they supervise, and in many ways this is the heart of the implementation effort. Consequently, monitoring is especially crucial at this level.

Implementation monitoring by supervisors consists of evaluating the timing and accomplishment of the elemental changes that contribute to task accomplishment, as well as evaluation of how well they work once they are in place. Implementation monitoring by managers consists of evaluating the timing and accomplishment of the operating level goals and how this supports and meshes with what is happening at the task level, based on information from the supervisors. Implementation monitoring by the monitor, and by leadership and the planning committee, consists of evaluating timing and accomplishment of the operating level goals in terms of how they support accomplishment of the strategic goals and, hence, the overall plan.

Supervisors often have difficulties evaluating task level change because they cannot tell whether apparent failure is due to the way the change is designed (including flaws in the operating level changes that are needed to support the task level change) or whether it is due to the inability of the person responsible for the change to make the change or make it work. They tend to attribute failures to people rather than to the change itself or to the situation. This often leads to censure of the individual when, in fact, he or she is blameless.

One reason that individuals are blamed for change failure is that it often is their behavior that signals that something is wrong. That is, individuals usually can tell that the change for which they are responsible is not working out. Rather than reporting the failure, they either plug away in vain or simply stop trying. In either case, the outcome is failure to produce results, missed deadlines, complaining, apparent uncooperativeness, absenteeism, and complaints from coworkers about their inability to depend on the individual or on the timeliness of the individual's output. Of course, these symptoms may reflect either flaws in the design of the change or a loss of motivation or both. The supervisor must figure out what is wrong and attempt to fix it.

The best way of discriminating is to examine the individual at work. If he or she is sincerely trying but is doing things wrong, training is in order. If he or she is sincerely trying, and is doing things that ought to work but do not, then the change probably is poorly designed or the operating structure does not support the change; the individual is not at fault. If the individual is not trying, however, or has simply given up without reporting the difficulty to the supervisor, something must be done.

An individual's failure to exert effort while expecting to be paid, or expecting to share in the reward the unit will get if it succeeds in spite of his or her failure to contribute, is called "free-riding." It may be unintentional: The individual is so frustrated by problems resulting from the change that he or she simply gives up. Or it may be intentional: The individual simply is unmotivated to work. Because supervisors tend to attribute poor results to the individual rather than the situation, their first impulse is to assume free-riding is intentional and to deal with it through coercion, special incentives (bribes), or prompting coworkers to exert social pressure. Coercion, usually the threat of being demoted or fired, is the most common response. Unfortunately, none of these responses works very well. If the individual is an intentional free-rider, coercion, incentives, and social pressure work only so long as they are applied; stop them and free-riding will reappear. If the individual is an unintentional free-rider, he or she cannot improve performance because of a lack of skills or because the change simply does not work. No amount of coercion, incentive, or social pressure will change the person's behavior. The change must itself be redesigned or the structure surrounding it must be revised to support it.

The reason for discussing free-riding is that the organization has to recognize it as a problem and help supervisors deal with it. Coercion, bribery, and social pressure are not long-term solutions. Supervisors and managers must be helped to avoid jumping to conclusions about the person being at fault before looking for situational causes. If it is concluded that the individual is in fact voluntarily free-riding, the problem should be turned over to the human resources department. If it is concluded that the free-riding is involuntary, then training, structural, or task issues must be addressed.

Investing in implementation monitoring. Monitoring is expensive because adding it to their other tasks spreads supervisors and managers very thin. Because of this, you must work with monitors to decide how much of their overall effort can be diverted to monitoring without detracting from their performance of their other tasks. Once this level of effort is determined, you must decide how to use it most effectively. *Effectiveness* can be described in terms of the thoroughness and frequency with which monitoring is done for a given level of investment of supervisor and manager effort.

Thoroughness means that the status of more than just the most salient changes is evaluated. Thoroughness requires the supervisor or manager to step back from the details of the implementation and to put things in perspective. Are we moving in the right direction? Are things working smoothly? Will tasks that are difficult now eventually become routine so they are less work? If we have problems, where are they? Can we solve them ourselves, or are they indicative of support or design flaws that should be addressed at a higher level?

The answers to these and similar questions must then be sifted so that the report to the monitor is succinct and useful. Gathering this information requires each manager or supervisor to consult with the various people in his or her unit and take the time to compose a report. It also requires honesty and willingness to report problems, which seldom comes easily when it may make the unit or the reporting person look bad.

All in all, this is a big job; it cannot be done on the run, and it cannot be done superficially. It requires that the supervisor or manager expend time, energy, and brainpower if it is to be done properly. Most supervisors and managers are used to making reports to their superiors, but this kind of report requires an unusual degree of honesty and willingness to risk looking bad if it is to be useful in monitoring the progress of plan implementation.

Frequency means how often evaluations and reports are made. Consider the swimmer who must occasionally interrupt the routine of swimming to look up and take bearings to gage progress toward the finish line. Increased frequency of checking progress assures greater accuracy because it permits timely correction of deviations from the most efficient path, but it exacts the price of interrupting the flow of swimming (implementation).

Effort means the amount of overall supervisory and managerial time and work withdrawn from other tasks and diverted to monitoring. There probably is no limit to the amount of effort that could be put into monitoring. There is always a better, faster, more accurate way to update information about progress. There has to be a limit, however, to how much will be invested, or monitoring will consume everything, bleeding resources from implementation and everything else. Theoretically, the point at which the cost of any more monitoring would start to undercut implementation is the level of effort that is appropriate for that particular implementation. Practically, the amount of available resources determines the level of effort that actually is devoted to monitoring.

Tradeoff means that thoroughness and frequency of monitoring can be differentially emphasized as implementation progresses. This is because infrequent but thorough monitoring can detect small or obscure signs of impending difficulties, permitting corrective steps to be taken before anything dire occurs. On the other hand, frequent but less thorough monitoring can detect glaring difficulties almost as soon as they arise and can trigger remedial action. Therefore, although there are obviously exceptions at the margin, as a general rule thoroughness and frequency can be traded off for any given level of effort you are willing to invest.

The relative amounts of thoroughness and frequency of monitoring for any level of effort is determined by the nature of the plan that is being implemented. Plans vary in their complexity, their clarity, and their pleasantness. A *complex* plan has many goals, and many changes are required to achieve those goals. Complexity also includes the need for coordination of changes across tasks and units and the need for some changes having been made prior to other changes being made. Complexity necessarily increases the need for interunit and intraunit communications in addition to more complex reporting to the monitor.

A *clear* plan may or may not be complex. If the relationships between tasks can be clearly defined and if people can comprehend their roles in the overall scheme, even a complex plan can be clear. On the other hand, if people are tentative about what is required of them, about the person to whom they report, or about how to do the tasks that they perceive to be assigned to them, even a very straightforward plan can be unclear.

A plan is *unpleasant* when its implementation is stressful and demanding, although it promises generous rewards in the future. Thus, if the plan requires employees to make great changes in what they do, to learn new skills, to move to new units, or to put in longer hours, it may be unpleasant. Most of all, a plan that is not wholly compatible with the culture is unpleasant; people are uncomfortable with it and consequently are under stress.

Because the amount of effort allocated to monitoring tends to be fixed, it seldom is possible to invest in both very frequent and very thorough monitoring. The question is what combination of the two is best, given the circumstances. The general rule is that the more complex, less clear, and more unpleasant the plan is, the *greater* the need for frequent monitoring, which requires diversion of effort from thorough monitoring. Conversely, when the plan is simple, clear, and pleasant, less frequent but more thorough monitoring is in order—if you don't do it often, you have to do it well when you do it. The task is to select the mix to fit the circumstances.

Of course, contingencies are seldom at either extreme. More lenient contingencies permit less extreme mixes of thoroughness and frequency. Also, the mix seldom remains the same throughout; different phases of the plan require different mixes and different units may require different mixes. On the other hand, when problems are encountered or particularly sensitive phases of implementation are undertaken, it is common to increase the resource (effort) allocation so both frequency and thoroughness can be increased.

Strategic Monitoring

Strategic monitoring relies on three kinds of information. The first is provided by the monitor, who reports about implementation progress. The second is provided by the mechanism you have in place for ongoing assessment of the organization's external and internal environments. The third is provided by measures of the organization's performance. Often the latter are the same measures the organization has traditionally gathered for its annual reports and other summaries of its overall performance.

It is the leadership team's job to reconcile these three kinds of information. As implementation proceeds, the organization should begin to move toward coping with its threats and opportunities, imperceptibly at first, but more rapidly as implemented changes take hold. This means that performance measures should begin to reflect those changes as performance addresses the threats and opportunities (which, you recall, are moving targets). It takes insight and clear thinking to judge whether performance is effectively addressing threats and opportunities because there is no one-to-one correspondence between the way in which threats are measured and the way in which performance is measured. This is largely a judgment call and, as such, is subject to wishful thinking. This is the time for clear-eyed, critical thinking and total honesty. If things are going well, fine. If not, something must be done: appropriate midcourse changes in the various levels of the plan and renewed effort at timely implementation.

In large part, strategic monitoring relies on milestones that are imbedded in the plan (Chapter 4). Milestones are levels of performance that the designers of the plan decided would indicate appropriate strategic progress. For businesses, milestones are usually expressed in terms of sales, profits, cash flow, market share, stock price, and similar measures of profitability and value relative to the specific threats and opportunities in their environments. For other organizations, milestones are expressed in terms of amounts raised through fund drives or successful grant applications, number of clients served, increases in membership, expressed satisfaction on the part of constituents, and so on.

Selection of appropriate measure is very difficult. Unfortunately, numeric measures often are selected for their convenience rather than for their real value as indicators of progress toward goals. Thus, schools are sometimes evaluated on the basis of their students' achievement test scores, although any thoughtful person would concede that such scores do not give a complete picture of a school's success. Welfare agencies sometimes are evaluated in terms of how many clients they serve, not in terms of how well they serve them. Colleges sometimes are evaluated by how many of their students get jobs immediately after graduation, not by the quality of the students' lives as a result of receiving an education. In short, there is a strong tendency to use easily quantified evaluations as milestones, even when they do not provide a useful picture of what is going on.

Some organizations have tried to add "soft," or qualitative, measures of progress to the "hard," or quantitative, measures that they customarily use. For example, surveys of client, customer, or employee satisfaction often are used. The problem with these measures is that they require more care than hard measures do; people approach questionnaires from many different viewpoints and, unless the questions are very carefully selected, the information obtained may be more misleading than not. Satisfaction is a particularly difficult variable because people tend to give such extreme answers. That is, they are either very satisfied or very unsatisfied, and the middle ground does not show up as often as one might expect. When it does, the responses may merely indicate indifference.

Knowing When to Stop

Closely tied to strategic monitoring is the question of knowing when to stop the implementation of a plan. The simple answer, of course, is that one should stop when one reaches the strategic goals or when it is clear that things are hopeless and it is time to consider a completely different strategy for survival. There are, however, two difficulties. First, many plans never attain their strategic goals because the goals change so much over time that what was sought at the beginning is not what is sought later on (threats and opportunities are moving targets). In this case, it may be time to stop implementing the existing plan and move on either to evolutionary change that keeps abreast of the moving targets or to a different plan for revolutionary change. Second, when a plan fails to attain its goals, people hesitate to walk away and sacrifice the resources that they already have spent on it; they keep hoping that by trying a little harder and spending a little more, they eventually can succeed.

Changing Goals

Goals, and plans, may change so much over time that the organization never really reaches them. As opportunities and threats arise, goals become outmoded and new ones take their place, often without any real recognition that the vision is being modified. Indeed, the process is often so subtle that everyone is surprised when they go back and realize where they have been and where they find themselves going. In some cases, the old goals came and went without fanfare, and one could even argue that they were reached, but by the time it happened, they were not of much interest anymore. In other cases, the old goals simply faded away and were replaced by more pressing goals. The process simply evolved. And, of course, in some cases, there were recognizable changes, even revolutions, and old goals were deliberately tossed out and replaced by new ones.

Sunk Costs

It seldom is apparent that a plan is failing early in its implementation. Rather, problems tend to arise along the way, often so small at first that nobody really notices because they are intent on getting the job done. By the time it becomes clear that things are not going well, large amounts of money and work have been expended (called "sunk costs"), and the leaders face a huge dilemma: "Should we shut down the plan and prevent further losses, or should we pour in more resources in an effort to make this thing work?"

One might think that as the situation becomes more hopeless and is increasingly recognized as such, that the plan would be dropped and another adopted in its place. Too often, exactly the opposite happens. Even when they know that the plan is faulty, organizations' leaders and members often continue with it, pouring more and more resources into it in an attempt to snatch victory from the jaws of defeat. Their rationale is that they do not want to "waste" the resources that already have been sunk into the plan. The idea is that perhaps investment of just a little more, and then a little more, and then a little more, will do the trick. An economist would urge them to look to the future rather than the past, to regard spent resources as gone and to focus on what they can expect to gain by proper use of future resources. But organizations, particularly their leaders, have difficulty abandoning the resources they have sunk into the implementation and tend to divert resources from elsewhere in order to continue with the plan—this is called "escalation of commitment" (Staw & Ross, 1987). After it becomes clear that there are more downs than ups and that the trend is downward, stalling action is taken: Expenses are cut; people are laid off; and other activities are cut back in order to provide resources for continued implementation of the plan. Sometimes these actions have a positive effect, but often they do not. If the plan is fundamentally flawed, the problem lies in persisting with it; giving it more resources will not provide a remedy.

Hope and fear. Hope and fear are the dark side of persistence: hope that persisting will lead to success and fear that failing to persist will result in even greater, unknown difficulties. In pressing either for staying with the plan or abandoning it, hope and fear tend to distort perception and blunt the impact of information. Hope promotes wishful thinking. Fear promotes "catastrophizing" (seeing the threat of failure in everything). Neither contributes to the clear thinking that good monitoring requires.

Barriers to Stopping

It is interesting that leaders who come into an organization that is implementing a failing plan seldom have difficulty stopping it and adopting a new vision and plan. Apparently, because they are not responsible for the "bad investment," they feel less bound to carry through. This observation provides a clue as to why the other leaders, those who are responsible for the sunk costs, are less inclined to forsake things. Leaders are rewarded for persistence and for overcoming obstacles, and the failure of a plan is seen by them (and by others) as a personal failure of leadership. This can result in penalties, even removal from leadership, and the accompanying loss of money, prestige, and self-esteem. Examples of leaders who persisted in the face of adversity, Winston Churchill in World War II and Lee Iacocca in the auto industry argued for perseverance. Failure is a leader's greatest enemy, although logic indicates that it sometimes must happen.

Leadership is not always at fault. Large organizations have an inertia that keeps their activities moving on courses that leaders may want to change but that are difficult to turn around. The analogy is often made between turning a large organization and turning a large ship in a stormy sea—there is a long time between the decision and the final result. Moreover, the politics of organizations often gets in the way. Even if a plan is not meeting the goals of the organization as a whole, it may well be meeting the goals of some units within the organization or of coalitions of organization members. If a group is fighting for power, failure of the plan may well be exactly what they need to bring down the present leaders and assert their right to take over.

The organization's culture also may present a barrier to stopping implementation of a failing plan. If quitting is scorned, or if some aspect of the plan is particularly congruent with the culture, it is difficult to give it up. For example, when steel manufacturers hit hard times, they debated about whether to move out of the steel business and into more promising businesses. Such a move was unthinkable to many "steel men" because steel was the only business they knew. It always had been the heart of the business and was central to the culture.

A Test

How then is a leader to distinguish "right-minded" persistence from "wrong-minded" escalation of commitment to a losing plan? Staw and Ross (1987) suggest five tests:

1. Is it difficult to define what constitutes failure? If so, it is easy to slip into misplaced hope and escalation of commitment.

2. Would I think less of myself if the plan failed? A symptom is that I fear the effects of failure on my career and self-esteem more than I fear the effects of failure on the organization.

3. Do I have difficulty interpreting feedback about the plan, particularly negative feedback? One symptom is that I think less of people who voice doubts about success and more of people who tell me what I hope is true.

4. Do I tend to favor the plan and its success over everything else in the organization? A symptom is that I look at the impacts of proposals and events on the plan before I look at their impacts on other activities.

5. Do I sometimes feel that if this project ends, there is nothing to look forward to?

In short, you, the leader, must ask yourself whether you would recognize failure if it occurred, because if you cannot recognize it, you never will know when to stop. You must ask how ego-involved you are in the success of the plan and whether you will take its failure so personally that failure is unthinkable. You must ask yourself if you are distorting information and whether you tend to "shoot the messenger" who brings bad news. You must ask whether the plan looms so high in your thinking that it overshadows other aspects of the organization's functioning. Perhaps it should be given first priority, but this should be a conscious decision, and the implications of that decision must be thought through. Finally, if you see the plan as the be-all and end-all, as the sole way in which the organization can move, alternatives are automatically ruled out. This means that there is no course other than complete commitment to the plan. Complete commitment implies provision of resources until the well runs dry. Of course, the well may, in fact, run dry, damaging the entire organization.

What do you do if you fail the test? First, of course, you should start talking to both your allies and your critics to obtain their views about the plan's progress and whether escalation of commitment already has begun. That is, opinions must be sought outside the tight circle of one's friends and advisors. They probably have as much to lose as you do by stopping implementation, so they are not objective observers. Your critics may be harsh, but they may be helpful.

If things look bad, there is little to do but bite the bullet. Admitting that things are not going well before someone else publicly makes the point gives you the advantage, but this works best if the admission can be accompanied by an alternative plan. There are many examples of leaders being able to step back, see that a new direction is needed, and then propose one. Often, however, before this happens, other forces such as the organization's members or the firm's shareholders have taken steps, usually resulting in the leader's removal, so his or her proposals are never given a chance.

Sometimes, however, graceful admission of failure and proposal of new directions can save your career. But this must be merely a prelude to serious work—a reexamination of the vision and the plan and judicious selection of new goals and new ways of reaching them. In short, this requires setting the organization in a new direction. This is hard work, even harder than it would be for a new leader who had not helped design the old vision and the old plan, who had not put work and time into the failed implementation, and who does not have to regain credibility and respect. It is, however, work that must be done, and unwillingness to do it constitutes a greater fault than unwillingness to stop implementation of the failing plan.

Success

Knowing when to stop is sometimes difficult when the plan succeeds, but less so than when it fails. Success means that the organization is in the position to keep abreast of threats and opportunities; it has the resources and mechanisms for thwarting the former and exploiting the latter. You might think your job is done, but of course it is not. You now must turn to making sure the organization does not backslide, does not regress toward its earlier state. This requires you to undertake making the changes permanent, the new "normal." In Chapter 6, we will see how this is done.   .

Steller Again

Before moving on, let us revisit our fictionalized company, Steller Art Frames, and its leader, The Mighty Carson. Recall that the vision and plan adopted by Steller was to increase production and profits by expanding production and reaching new markets. Specifically, the idea was to use Steller's experienced supervisors as trainers for a new workforce in Mexico and in a local enterprise zone, to expand the product line to include art deco and art nouveau frames for the American market, and to link with a

European distributor to market mission-style frames in Germany, Austria, and Scandinavia. In addition, Steller would expand its business to include licensing of its patented fastening system.

Carson took the lead in the implementation, although details were in the hands of the implementation committee. Her first problem before selling Steller's building was to borrow enough money to see Steller through the first phase of its transition, which was difficult because the company already was in financial trouble. Banks were unwilling to help, so she turned to her European marketing partner, finally borrowing enough to get started and obtaining a promise of more if things looked promising.

The borrowed money was used to lease and remodel facilities in Mexico (a section of a building formerly housing a chainsaw assembly plant) and purchase the necessary equipment. Recruitment of Mexican workers went poorly at first because the implementation committee insisted that only cabinetmakers would have the necessary qualifications to make high-quality mission-style frames. It turned out that Steller could not pay competitive wages for cabinetmakers, so they had to settle for workers with carpentry experience, which turned out just fine. An initial group of 30 eager new workers was brought to Steller's home offices for training. Meanwhile, a consultant had been working with Steller's frame makers to design a formal training program and teach them training techniques. Although production continued during all of this, it sometimes seemed to Carson that the company was bleeding money.

After the Mexican plant was up and running, Carson sold Steller's building and used the proceeds to move the company to remodeled space in an old warehouse in the enterprise zone and to purchase state-of-the-art equipment for making picture frames. Recruitment from among the zone's targeted pool of unemployed young people began even before the new equipment was fully installed. The bright spot in all of this was the ease with which the art deco and art nouveau frames were put into production. This was because Jimmy, the would-be designer, went to the local library and checked out books from which he compiled the most common deco and nouveau design elements. Then he adapted Steller's copyrighted mission-style designs, using his new collection of design elements. The result was truly brilliant; the adaptations were both handsome and easy to set up for production, even with a workforce less skilled than Steller was used to having. Carson was so impressed that she gave Jimmy a bonus and put him in charge of all of Steller's design work.

Things continued to improve when Carson found a way for the gilding machine purchased by Poor Wayne to pay for itself. Although it was of lower quality than the gilding being done by hand in Mexico, the gold and silver made the deco and nouveau frames distinctive and very classy. In addition, Carson decided to put the machine's high productivity to use making lengths of gold and silver stock for sale to framing shops, a market that Steller had never served before.

After securing its patent rights, Carson made it known that Steller was interested in licensing its fastener system. Within days, she had entered into negotiation with a very large furniture manufacturing company that offered even better terms than she had anticipated. They quickly concluded a nonexclusive arrangement that allowed Steller to license to other manufacturing companies outside the furniture industry. Before long a second arrangement was made with a window frame manufacturer, and then a third was made with a maker of prefabricated bathroom and kitchen cupboards.

Steller's implementation followed the guidelines outlined in this chapter, adapted to its unique needs. One unanticipated benefit was that Carson's secretary (now called an administrative assistant) undertook the review of 80 years' worth of documents that had been stored in boxes in the basement of the old building. From these, she pieced together both a history of the Steller company and a set of documents that were appropriate for the new way the company was going to work.

On the other hand, nearly every timeline was missed. The Mexican facilities and the move to the enterprise zone both took longer than anticipated. This was in large part because personnel cuts by Carson's predecessor left too little slack to allow the administrative staff to keep up with their jobs while implementing the plan. This meant that Carson had to use some of her dwindling funds to hire temporary workers. Even at that, stress remained high, and Carson found herself resolving conflicts and calming flared tempers.

Overall, however, everyone knew that once implementation had begun, there was no going back. This was a life or death battle. So they pitched in, although a few people resisted having to leave longtime coworkers when they found themselves moved to new divisions. And six people quit, two of whom were immediately hired by a local company that made "rustic" furniture. It turned out that "rustic" was code for "poorly made" and, disgusted, the two employees returned to Steller. The other four vacancies were filled by people who had previously left the company and now wanted to be part of its renewal.

After the Mexican facility was ready, Carson took all the U.S. employees to the opening ceremony and a reception afterwards with the local Mexican officials. Later, when the implementation committee felt that things were pretty well in place for the company as a whole, Carson brought the Mexican employees in for a huge companywide celebration. It cost a bundle (dinner and dancing at a country club), but it served to signal that Steller was over the hump in implementing its plan. Now it was a matter of working hard and waiting to see how things turned out.

Summary

To aid in mastery of this material, summarize it for yourself by filling in this topic outline.

Implementation: Producing Change

  I. Cheerleading

 II. Monitoring
    A. What is monitored?
    B. Implementation monitoring
       1. Investing in implementation monitoring
    C. Strategic monitoring

III. Knowing when to stop
    A. Changing goals
    B. Sunk costs
       1. Hope and fear
    C. Barriers to stopping
    D. A test
    E. Success

Exercises

1. Once again, interview your current or retired organization leader, this time asking questions about plan implementation. To what degree, and in what ways, did the plan change between its inception and its completion? What were the problems that arose, and how they were addressed? Were there difficulties with free-riders, and if so, what was done about them? How was monitoring accomplished? Was the plan fully implemented? If not, why not?

2. Ask similar questions of your other interviewees with an eye to how their views differ from those of the leader.

3. Write an essay on implementation that outlines your viewpoint and add it to your notebook.

Sources and Further Reading

Alexander, L. D. (1985). Successfully implementing strategic decisions. *Long Range Planning, 18,* 91–97.

Bissell, B. L. (1992). *Relationship between incongruity of supervisory strategy and satisfaction with the organization and/or supervision.* Unpublished doctoral dissertation. University of Arizona, Tucson.

Dauten, D. A. (1980). *Quitting: Knowing when to leave.* New York: Walker.

Nutt, P. C. (1986). Tactics of implementation. *Academy of Management Journal, 29,* 230–261.

Nutt, P. C. (1987). Identifying and appraising how managers install strategy. *Strategic Management Journal, 8,* 1–14.

Samuelson, W., & Zeckhauser, R. (1988). Status quo bias in individual decision making. *Journal of Risk and Uncertainty, 1,* 7–59.

Silver, W. S., & Mitchell, T. R. (1990, Spring). The status quo tendency in decision making. *Organizational Dynamics, 34*–46.

Sproull, L. S., & Hoffmeister, K. R. (1986). Thinking about implementation. *Journal of Management, 12,* 43–60.

Staw, B. M., & Ross, J. (1987, March). Knowing when to pull the plug. *Harvard Business Review, 68*–74.

Six

Follow-Through: Institutionalizing Change

*Prime Responsibility # 6: Leaders must work with others
to institutionalize achieved changes and to help members accept
ongoing change as a normal aspect of the organization and its activities.*

Implementation is winding down. You have been monitoring things closely, and it is clear that the strategic goals are going to be reached as implemented changes kick in. Things generally look good. Of course, nothing this big ever works out quite the way it was supposed to. The vision changed in the course of implementation: some parts of the plan failed to produce desired results, and other parts produced unexpected results. But remedies were made, and it truly looks like the plan has successfully addressed the external and internal threats and opportunities. The next challenge is to follow through to make sure the good news stays good.

Four Tasks

There are four follow-through tasks involved in institutionalizing change: communication, document updating, aligning the reward structure, and making sure the organization's culture incorporates both the specific changes that have been made and the belief that continuing change is desirable and normal.

Communication

The first task in the institutionalizing process focuses on convincing the organization's members and relevant outsiders that things are better for having undergone change. This means convincing them that things are better than they were or that things are better than they would have been had changes not been made. The goal is to create a willingness to continue with the new practices rather than merely regard them as a temporary departure from the familiar, normal way things were before. It also is to create a willingness to regard change as an ongoing feature of life, thereby reducing inertia when the next wave of change is undertaken.

The essence of this first task is frequent and repeated communication, making sure the communications all tell a consistent story about what has been accomplished. One way to ensure consistency is to construct an "official history" of what has happened.[1] Beginning with why change was necessary, it should include the vision and how and why that vision was crafted, the master plan and how it fit with the vision, the goals that drove the plan, and the steps that were taken to implement the plan. If the plan was altered in midstream to accommodate changing conditions, those alterations and their rationale should be described. Finally, the outcomes of implementation should be described. Your monitoring efforts during implementation will provide the data you need (numbers always are important when describing successes).

This official history must then be the basis of all communications with the organization's various constituencies. You, as leader, must undertake a campaign of communicating the successes of the change initiative and the prospects for those aspects that are still in progress. Other members of the management structure should base their communications on the history so everyone is telling the same story, thus keeping everything focused and clear.

It is, of course, absolutely necessary that this history and your communications be accurate and credible. It will be tempting to embellish the history and inflate the successes, but remember your audience knows a lot about what has been going on, and they will react to hyperbole and error by rejecting the whole story. In fact, you may never convince some percentage of that audience that the initiative was necessary, desirable, or successful. These folks will always long for the good old days. Even if they cooperated during implementation, they never really bought into change, and they still expect that when the dust settles, things will get back to normal. Disgruntled people often have a good deal of influence on their peers, so they are dangerous. It is only by convincing the over-whelming majority that change was a good thing that these voices can be drowned out and the changes can become accepted as the new "normal."

The good news is that you have a powerful psychological principle working for you. It has long been known that when people take an active part in some activity, particularly if they publicly support it, their initial negative attitudes toward it shift toward being more positive. This may not bring the hard-core dissidents into the fold, but it will shift many of the people who doubted but were willing to participate and see how things came out. Everyone who was involved in implementing the changes has invested considerable mental and physical effort. This investment tends to make them want to think that it was all worthwhile. It is the your job, in concert with the other members of the leadership and management team, to make it clear that what they want to believe is, in fact, true: The effort was worthwhile.

Document Updating

The second task in institutionalizing change is to bring all of the organi-zation's documentation into line with the new state of affairs. We have not discussed the (usually underappreciated) role of documents in the smooth functioning of an organization. That would take another book. Suffice it to say that documents (properly done in the first place, kept current, and actually consulted) are the organization's memory bank. Without them, everyone marches to his or her own drummer. Important information must be passed by word of mouth, and management has no idea if what is being passed is either accurate or helpful. Documents provide an official record that helps clarify what has been said. Most organizations' documentation is poorly organized and out of date. This is unfortunate because current and accessible documentation can help the organization function more smoothly and efficiently.

Document updating during the institutionalization of change not only provides a written record of where things stand, it also provides an internal audit of how well the activities of the various parts of the organization—from individual members and their responsibilities to the larger units—are aligned in pursuit of the organization's goals and vision. That is, it can help you tell whether change has permeated the organization, as reflected in the activities of its units and members. It may seem like a great deal of work to do this audit and document update, but it provides you with an invaluable picture of what is going on throughout the organization.

How this task is carried out depends on the size and resources of the organization. It can be daunting if the organization is big; less so if it is small. The expense is proportional. Just as you had to decide how much to invest in implementation monitoring, you must decide how much effort and money can be expended on document update, as well as about the level of detail you need. The effort proceeds in two phases, and the first phase consists of four steps:

1. You and the other leaders of the organization must sit down and reexamine the vision and mission statement that were written at the beginning of the change initiative. In light of intervening events, they may no longer be precisely accurate, and now is the time to revise them. Goals that were achieved can be evaluated in terms of their actual contribution to the vision, in contrast to their hoped-for contribution at the beginning of the initiative. In contrast to the history of the change effort, the focus here is on the present state of things: a clear statement about where the organization is and what it is doing.

2. This statement is then passed to the next level of management. Middle level managers should take the statement compiled by top management (the leadership team) and evaluate how well their units' activities fit with it. There will be a tendency to force a fit in order to look good, but this should be discouraged by pointing out that inaccuracies will come to light when subsequent information from supervisors and employees does not confirm them. The purpose is to see if the units' activities reflect the change of direction that has been the goal of all these months of work. If they do not, or if parts of what they do fail to reflect change but should, the unit heads should devise a plan for bringing things into alignment. It will be necessary to follow up to make sure these plans are implemented and that they do the job.

3. After middle level managers have done their work, supervisors should be asked to describe how their subunits' activities fit with the

evolving document. Again, where there is a lack of fit, supervisors, in cooperation with their managers, should be asked to implement remedies, with appropriate follow up.

4. Finally, all employees (including you) should describe how their activities contribute to their subunits' activities. This can be done in the form of an updated job description.

The second phase of documentation update consists of your consultants, or whoever is overseeing this effort, sitting down with all the information and integrating it with the goal of seeing how the activities (job descriptions) of individual employees contribute to the activities of their subunits, how the activities of the subunits contribute to the activities of the units, and how the activities of the units contribute to the activities of the organization as a whole. Anomalies must be tagged for further examination or even intervention if they reveal nonproductive or unaligned activities.

This can be a huge undertaking, and it is fraught with error. Everybody at every level has reason to make things look better than they probably are. Even the best intended people color the truth if there is a possibility of negative consequences. You simply have to accept this; the picture this process yields is not so much a realistic portrait as it is a rough sketch. But a rough sketch may be all you need, and even a rough sketch is more than you have if you do not do this at all. Moreover, if the people who perform the work do so with sensitivity and care, the results will be good enough to help you understand how substantially the changes have permeated the organization, from top to bottom. This knowledge, together with further assessment of the organization's external environment, allows you to pinpoint where further change is needed.

A great deal of the value of the document update process derives from the descriptions of what they do that are provided by individual employees at every level of the organization. The odds are that the job descriptions in your old documentation were out of date, inaccurate, and incomplete even before the change initiative, so they are bound to be even worse now that changes have altered people's jobs. The old descriptions probably consist of a few hackneyed phrases put together with a minimum of reflection simply to satisfy the requirement to submit a completed form. Frankly, almost nobody outside of the human resources department actually knows how to write a job description, least of all the job's incumbent.

On the other hand, people who cannot write a job description that even vaguely conveys the essence of what they do can talk for hours about their job to a willing listener. Because their jobs fill such a large part of their waking hours, most people identify closely with them and are happy to discuss them when given the opportunity. This suggests that asking people to write a job description is likely to be less profitable than asking them to describe what they do to a willing listener. The problem is finding a willing listener who has the human resource training to convert the verbal description to a written job description. And having found such a person, there is the expense of using him or her for every employee in the organization. It is far better to interview a subset of the people in each unit, selecting interviewees from different job classifications in the unit. These job descriptions can then be distributed (with proper precautions for privacy) to uninterviewed employees with similar jobs. They can revise the descriptions to fit their own unique jobs rather than start from scratch or merely tinker with their old inadequate job descriptions. The advantage of doing things this way is that the interviewer can focus on those aspects of the jobs that should be aligned with the new changes, asking appropriate questions when such information is not spontaneously provided.

When this work is completed, documents can be updated to reflect what was found. The first update will be in job descriptions, which has far-reaching training and hiring implications. Then operating procedures must be changed to bring them into alignment with the organization's new aims. For example, it may be found that rules and support for computer use must be revised to encourage behavior that is aligned with the new changes. Or hiring priorities may need revision. Or procedures for dealing with customer service may have to be rewritten. In short, all of the organization's various rules, policies, and procedures, at every level, must be examined and updated as required.

Realigning Rewards

It is amazing how many organizations strive to achieve one thing while rewarding people for doing something else entirely. Until rather recently, university presidents exhorted faculty to improve teaching but made pay raises contingent on research productivity. It took years for administrators to face the fact that people treat rewards as messages: If the rewards favor activity B, then that must be what truly is important, despite rhetoric about the importance of activity A.

Similarly, you must have the right reward structure if you want employees' activities to support the changes an organization has undergone. When an organization undergoes change, some activities that formerly were valued will diminish in value, and some (or new activities) will increase in value. In order to communicate the new value structure and in order to ensure that valued activities receive priority, the organization's reward structure must reflect those values.

You can think of rewards as tokens that are given to employees or groups of employees to help them understand the organization's priorities and to encourage them to act in accordance with those priorities. There are three categories of tokens, each aimed at a slightly different audience:

1. Status—recognition, advancement, preference in transfers, titles, prestigious work space (e.g., an office with a window), greater responsibility, an assistant, centrality and power through membership in crucial decision-making and policy bodies, highly visible special job assignments. Using status as a reward is a very public way of telling both the recipient and others in the organization that the organization values the variety and quality of the activities in which the recipient has engaged. Although the goal is to motivate the recipient to keep up the good work, it also is to instruct and encourage observers to do likewise. Thus we give awards and plaques and recognition dinners so models of proper behavior can be identified and others can see what they should be doing in the hope that they too can earn such rewards.

2. Job resources—increased budget, better work space, more personnel, updated equipment, a new company car. Job resources often are given to a unit or part of a unit in recognition of the importance of their function and the quality of their performance. This is somewhat less public than awarding status, and the resources usually are shared by all the people in the unit. But the reward communicates to both the recipients and outsiders that the unit's activities are valued and that it is a good idea to try to earn such rewards for their own units. Often the head of a rewarded unit derives considerable satisfaction from this kind of reward, although he or she derives little from it personally.

3. Personal resources—pay raises, bonuses, benefits. This often is the least public form of reward because many organizations are secretive about how much people get paid. Strangely, the effects of a raise or a bonus often are less lasting than the effects of receiving public recognition and a

$20 plaque. Nearly everyone thinks they ought to be paid more, so unless an increase is stunningly large, they generally accept it as their due and quickly adapt to it. The real impact of a raise depends on what it does to one's salary relative to what the person in the next office is making (or is assumed to be making). People think it is fair to be paid what others in similar jobs are paid, and if they are not, they become very unhappy. They look for jobs elsewhere when they think they are being treated unfairly. This means that if you give raises to reward performance, the difference between what the recipients are doing and what others are doing must be apparent to everyone. Otherwise the raise will be seen as unfair, not as a deserved reward. Pay fairness truly is shaky ground, and it is best to work with a compensation expert rather than take it upon yourself to hand out raises. Your good intentions can backfire, and it can be very expensive to put things right. In the long run, it usually is best to use one-time awards and bonuses rather than raises as rewards because they do not distort the perceived fairness of the organization's pay structure.

The fact is that all three of these categories of rewards account for only a small proportion of the effort that people put into their jobs. Happily, the work ethic is alive and well. Indeed, the work ethic, which includes self-reward for a job well done, is so powerful that it swamps the motivational effects of all but the most extreme external rewards. Although external rewards are necessary, they are not sufficient. As long as compensation is seen as distributed fairly, rewards serve primarily to highlight the organization's priorities so its members know where to apply their self-motivated work ethic.

The flip side of reward is punishment and the threat of punishment. Of course, every organization has rules with prescribed punishments for violating them. Properly documented and circulated (such as lists of things for which the organization's computers may not be used), rules and punishments clearly communicate the organization's priorities, just as rewards do, and therefore are useful to its members. Punishment for poor performance, on the other hand, often fails to communicate anything very clearly, except that something the person did or did not do fell short of a superior's expectations. This kind of punishment is counterproductive because it provides little guidance about what to do to avoid future punishment. I once worked with a football coach who could not understand why his players' performance did not improve when he "pointed out" their mistakes. In fact, all he did was shout and humiliate them when they failed. He didn't teach them what to do instead.

Although they are not quick to admit it, real or implied threat of punishment is part of every manager's arsenal. And, it works—at least in the short run. The problem with threat is that it produces grudging compliance rather than willing engagement. The desired activity usually stops when the threat stops, leading to even more dire threats. The whole thing tends to escalate, with the threats becoming more and more exaggerated until they become sheer bluff and the whole thing falls apart. Threat has to be used sparingly and subtly. It cannot promise cataclysm when nothing of the sort is likely to happen. The promise to withhold something that is desired, with the reason for doing so made clear, is about as extreme as most threats should ever be.

Punishment by cutting pay causes the same distortions in the organization's pay structure as raises do, and often invites legal action. Fines are the onetime counterpart of bonuses, but there has to be a clear, and legal, basis for imposing them, so they are not always a good idea.

The ultimate punishment is termination from the organization, and it is the last resort. It is one thing to lay people off because their job is no longer necessary (the procedures and legal issues usually are clear). It is another thing to fire them for poor performance. Documentation usually is required, and the process is time-consuming. In this litigious age, firing people can be so complicated that it should not be undertaken until all other avenues have been exhausted. But once the decision is made, it is best to proceed with deliberation and to get it done as quickly as possible. The longer the process draws on, the more disruptive it is for people's coworkers, and people are unlikely to do their job well, either through anger and spite or through preoccupation as they try to deal with what is happening to them.

Firing is extreme; it often induces a great deal of hardship for the person and his or her family, and it means that coworkers have to take on extra work until the job is filled with someone new. Moreover, like execution, it is final; there is no atoning for it if you subsequently find out you were wrong. When I was very young, I fired a woman for poor performance, only to find that I had to hire two people to replace her. There was no way on earth she could have done her job well. I had attributed the poor performance to her rather than to the way the job was structured, and I had made a wrong decision. Had I investigated as I should, I would have kept her and redesigned the job. I felt awful about firing her, and to make things even worse, she got another job in the same building, a job she really liked and where she was regarded as a real find. Whenever we met in the hallway, she would sincerely thank me for "prompting" her to move on to the new job—which once again reminded me of my mistake.

Culture Change

The previous three institutionalization tasks—communication, document updating, and reward alignment—are, in fact, aimed at promoting lasting changes in the organization's culture. To gage their success, some sort of assessment of the culture should be done, perhaps using the instrument in Appendix B, modified to acquire information specific to the changes that hopefully have occurred in the culture. Other kinds of questionnaires are likely to do the same thing, and it would be best if the questionnaire used before the change initiative (if there was one) could be re-administered to provide a before and after contrast. Your consultant or your human resources people ought to be able to design a suitable instrument if the one in Appendix B is too complicated.

The goal here is to see if the changes have become integrated into the culture or at least are beginning to be so. Do not be too disheartened if there is not much evidence of this at first. It takes time for cultures to change, and the best vehicle is familiarity with the changes that have been brought about. Familiarity comes with living with the new procedures and goals; as the threat of newness recedes, the culture will evolve. If the changes strike at a core, deeply held belief or value, however, the culture will be very slow to accept them, if it ever does. This may be troubling, but it is best that you know about it because it will be a continuing source of ill feeling and dissonance until the culture evolves or you decide to change the changes in deference to the culture. In the long run, however, research evidence suggests that people who are greatly upset about abridgment of deeply held beliefs and values will leave the organization if there is an opportunity to do so. New members who feel the same way will stay only a short time if they can move to an organization that has a more compatible culture. New members who can embrace the evolving culture will be comfortable in the organization and will stay as long as this comfort level persists.

What Happens Next?

Throughout these pages, we have proceeded as though the changes being made to your organization and its external environment are sizable and that the organization has had to undergo revolutionary change, devoting a great deal of work and resources to an intense and rather prolonged effort. In this chapter, we are assuming that these revolutionary changes are in place and the question is how to avoid having to undertake such an expensive and disruptive task again.

Large-scale change is necessitated by a gross misalignment between what the organization is doing and what it should be doing to survive and prosper. Usually this is because the organization's leaders have failed to continually assess the external and internal environments. By the time severe problems become obvious and the need for change becomes apparent, revolutionary change is the only available course.

In our new, postchange world, your job as leader is to make sure this does not happen again. That is, your job is to see that from now on the external and internal environments are continually assessed and that the changes needed to deal with events in those environments are undertaken in a timely manner. Quite simply, your job is to set the organization up for evolutionary change rather than repeated rounds of expensive, exhausting revolutionary change.

Of course, things will happen, both externally and internally, that will require quicker and more profound change than evolution can accommodate, but short of cataclysm, these minirevolutionary changes can be handled without undue upheaval if the organization is generally attuned to its environments. Smaller and more localized change initiatives are far easier to handle than wholesale makeovers of the entire organization, and they are far cheaper.

So now, this is the essence of your job:

1. Ease back on the rhetoric, so people can adapt to the revolutionary changes they have just been through.

2. Keep in place the mechanisms for assessing the external and internal environments, for updating the vision, for revising the plan, and for implementing change.

3. Make it clear in all that you say and do that ongoing change, albeit not revolutionary in size or effort, is a permanent feature of the organization and its future.

Sometimes leaders get so used to issuing calls to action and beating the drums of change that they forget to let up and let the dust settle. The result is that they try to keep the organization mobilized (with the expense and inefficiency implicit in that), and eventually people just stop listening. Trying to prolong a revolution that has run its course is a bad idea.

On the other hand, an organization that runs out of gas after a big change, that ceases to pay attention to its environments, that dismantles the mechanisms it has built to carry out change, is going to end up in another round of revolutionary change before long. This is bad because frequent bouts of extreme, revolutionary change exhaust everyone and lead the organization's members to lose faith in its leaders. This means that recovery time must be allowed, the environments must continue to be assessed, change mechanisms must be maintained, and the culture must accept that evolutionary change is the new norm, with revolutionary change occurring when it is necessary.

The best way to make continuous change part of the organization's culture is to be very straightforward about it in all communications. When celebrating success at the end of the big change initiative, you should make it clear that although the pace of change will slow, it will not stop. In everything you and other leaders and managers say and do, it should be explicitly stated that because the external and internal environments will always be in flux, the organization must continue to change accordingly. It must be made clear that the reason the organization has had to go through what it has just gone through is that it did not make the continuous changes it should have made. This need not be done in a way that makes previous leaders look foolish. But it should be done in a way that makes it clear that the new policy will be to make continuous change a way of life.

Never in all of this, however, should it be suggested that change is good in and of itself, because your audience knows better. Proportional to how extensive it is, change is expensive and difficult: Energy is diverted from necessary functions to making change happen, with the result that an organization undergoing major change seldom is very efficient. Resources are eaten up by change, often wasted because experiments fail or produce only small results. People have to work harder and longer as new systems and procedures are put in place and tested. Having been through even a reasonably modest change initiative, people have a pretty good idea what it takes, and they have little patience with change for change's sake.

Therefore, to retain credibility and to get people to accept that continuous change is desirable, you must make it clear that every change has a purpose: to meet specific challenges and clearly contribute to the organization's survival and prosperity. Remember, people crave security. Thus they must be helped to understand that security does not lie in routine and predictability. Instead, it lies in the flexibility and invention that ensures the organization's well-being and, in turn, their own well-being.

What Is Next For You?

As the revolution winds down, you probably will have conflicting emotions. On one hand, there is elation about success and pride in a job well done, as well as a sharp awareness of where things still fall short. On the other hand, there usually is bone-deep exhaustion and the desire to never again give the speech you have given hundreds of times. Elation and pride will energize you and make you want to start new projects and move new mountains; exhaustion and disgust with the sound of your own voice will argue for a long vacation. In the short run, the latter probably is the best idea.

After the vacation, or perhaps during it, you have to decide what is next for you. Leaders who are good at revolution often are not so good at evolution. You have to consider whether you are capable of continuing with the organization as an evolutionary leader or whether you would do best to set the organization up for evolution, leave it to someone else, and move to some other organization where your revolutionary experience can be put to good use.

On the other hand, most leaders have only a few revolutions in them. Revolutions take a huge physical and mental toll, and it is not clear that leaders actually get better at it as they get more experience. Perhaps undertaking the makeover of another organization is asking too much of yourself, and you should seriously consider turning yourself into an evolutionary leader. Or if you have the resources, maybe it is time retire and devote yourself to golf and good works. If you are young enough, and the prospect is appealing, you could go back to school, earn the proper credentials, and become a teacher: Pass on what you have learned to future leaders.

If you decide to leave the organization, you first must give some thought about who takes over when you go. Formally, this is called succession planning, but all it means is figuring out who among your immediate colleagues would be capable of taking over (and acceptable to others). Some organizations tend to promote from within, and succession planning makes good sense. Others tend to go outside for new leaders, which reduces succession planning to making a list of criteria for screening candidates to replace you.

If your organization's board or search committee is willing to consider replacing you with someone from within, you have the opportunity to influence the decision about who will carry on what you have started. Often the choice will be rather obvious; the person with whom you worked most closely during the revolution may be exactly right to succeed you. On the other hand, there may be a number of close colleagues, any one of whom might do a good job. It might be best to let somebody else, like the board or a selection committee, choose among them.

One problem with selecting someone from among the people who have had prominent roles in the revolution is that some of them will have been infected with what might be called "the revolution bug." That is, revolution tends to produce zealots, people who enjoy the energy and sense of mission that a revolution needs to succeed, and they like the idea of leaving their mark on the organization. Unfortunately, zealotry tends to be, if not blind, at least a little nearsighted. Zealots champion revolutionary change even when it may be unnecessary: "If you have an army, you should have a war!" Although one may admire their energy and commitment, they make it harder to convince the organization's members that continuous change is a good thing. Because it fails to distinguish between evolutionary and revolutionary change and tries to keep the organization mobilized and at fever pitch, zealotry offers exhaustion and chaos to people who yearn for a little peace and the time to consolidate gains already made. Boards and selection committees, impressed with the results of your revolution, may opt for someone who can carry on in the same vein. You may know that this is not a good thing, but it often is difficult to convince the people who will make the selection, and they may go for a zealot. You have to decide how dangerous you think this is and how much energy you are willing to expend in trying to prevent it. After all, it is your legacy that is at stake; you do not want things to fall apart the minute you leave.

The Question of Politics

You also have another legacy. Assuming you decide to stay and guide your organization through evolution punctuated with minirevolutions, you have to deal with the loose ends of your current revolution. The most profound of these is how to deal with your critics and your enemies.

Some of your critics will genuinely believe that your revolution was wrongheaded and that the organization has not gained by it. These people can be convinced by evidence and seldom are motivated by personal malice. Other critics are motivated by envy or a general aversion to authority figures; I do not know what you should do with them. Others use opposition to you and to the revolution to enhance their prestige and power among other dissenters. In the latter case, opportunism rather than malice motivates their stance, but they often get so caught up in their role that they can become quite vicious.

As long as critics remain civil and refrain from personal attacks, they can be assets because they make you and everyone else think carefully rather than just plunge ahead. But, when they move from criticism to public opposition, from reasoned argument to active confrontation, they become disruptive to the organization, and they become your enemies.

Enemies are an evitable product of having to make decisions that affect people's lives. Changes in organizations take power and resources from some and give them to others. Enemies are people who attribute real or imagined reversals of fortune to your decisions. If you are lucky, they will leave the organization. If you are unlucky, they will stay to fight what they perceive as error and injustice. Like it or not, if they declare war, you have no option but to respond.

Strangely enough, your response has to be more restrained than their attack. Everyone will see you as more powerful, so you must take care not to appear to be a bully. Your attackers also will see you as more powerful, and they therefore may feel justified in resorting to guerilla tactics such as scandal mongering, sabotage, or worse (tactics of which they might normally disapprove) in order to even things out. They see what they are doing as simple justice. Beware of people who begin arguments with, "It's the principle. . . ."

Having identified your enemies, you first should find out what has made them enemies. If an injustice truly has been done and if it is correctable, then it should be corrected and a sincere apology should be offered. If an injustice has been done but there is no way to correct it, a sincere apology may permit a truce. If an apology is insufficient or if you do not think the perceived injustice actually was an injustice, you must see things through to some sort of conclusion. Usually this consists of making the enemies less dangerous either by ejecting them from the organization or by isolating them within it. In either case, they may continue to work against you, but they can only do so from the periphery.

People often complain about the politics involved in organizations, as though they never encounter politics elsewhere. In fact, politics is simply the process by which people come to accommodate conflicting views and desires. It is a constant part of any interaction and is intensified by the size of the gains and losses (real and imagined) that ride on the outcomes. Politics is part of the human condition, and moaning about it changes nothing. It is far better to learn the rules and master the conventions. It is far better to know that you are embroiled in politics than to naively proceed on the assumption that good will and good intentions will prevail.

Celebrate Success

Whatever you decide about remaining with the organization, part of your efforts to clean up the loose ends of your revolution is to celebrate success. You, of course, understand how much remains to be done, the threats that lie on the horizon, the odds of regression toward the old norm. Nonetheless, celebration is important because it puts an official seal on the changes that have been made and thanks everyone for their buy-in and hard work.

Celebration is mostly communication. If the organization is small enough to get into one hall, a banquet is in order. After-dinner speeches should carry the message of success: generous thanks to all involved, recognition of those who bore the heaviest burden, and a vision of the future. If the organization is large, separate celebrations with its various units are in order, and if this is too much, at least you should distribute a videotape in which you give the speech you would have given had the organization been smaller.

Just a word about thanking people: You will be seen by many people, both within and outside the organization, as having single-handedly brought about successful change, perhaps even as having single-handedly saved the organization. Enjoy the adulation, but don't take it too seriously. True, you worked hard, but the real nitty-gritty of making the changes and making them work was done by people throughout the organization; recall that your role was largely cheerleading.

Therefore, your remarks at the various ceremonies at which you are honored should be humble and emphasize the contributions of others. Accepting praise is tricky; you must come off as modest but not so modest that you look phony. You need not deny your role in making the organization better, but you should graciously share the credit. It is a good idea to rehearse what you are going to say and get a trusted opinion about how well you balance pride and modesty.

Celebration is easy when threats have been thwarted or turned to opportunities and when opportunities have been exploited and the organization clearly is better off than it was before. It is hard when the evidence for success is less obvious.

Recall the ancient joke about a man who always left his friends with the benediction, "May your house be safe from tigers." This was puzzling because he lived in North America. When asked, he said he did this because it obviously worked: His friends' houses had never been attacked by tigers. Insofar as it's funny, this joke turns on the problem of affirming or disconfirming a proposition on the basis of the failure of an event to occur. Unfortunately, it has parallels with the problem of affirming the success when changes successfully prevented an anticipated threat from occurring.

The purpose of undertaking large-scale change is to thwart an existing or anticipated external or internal threat or to exploit an existing or anticipated external or internal opportunity. Success is fairly obvious if an existing, clearly recognized threat is thwarted or an existing, clearly recognized opportunity is exploited. This is particularly true if the organization's competitors fall victim to the threat or fail to take advantage of the opportunity; the contrast with your organization's experience is testimony to the efficacy of its efforts to make the right changes.

On the other hand, success is more difficult to define when change successfully eliminates anticipated threats before they occur. It is not always clear that the anticipated threats actually would have materialized; efforts to avoid or counter them may have been needless. It really is hard to answer critics in this situation. You launched a preemptive change initiative, convinced people it was necessary because of the anticipated threat, and the threat never occurred. Did the change effort avert the threat, or was whole thing just a false alarm? Critics will charge that the sky never was in danger of falling because—Behold!—it never fell. Things could have gone on as they were, and money spent on change and all the work that went into it could have been used to better purpose.

A somewhat similar situation exists for opportunities. Success often is defined as making things better than they were before. But this may be asking too much. Sometimes merely failing to regress is progress. In a very competitive industry or in a very tumultuous environment, acting on opportunities may not advance the organization, but it may keep it from falling behind. When drowning is imminent, just keeping your head above water counts as a victory.

In both of these cases, celebration of success requires some prior spadework. Unless you can clearly demonstrate that change nullified a threat or kept the organization from falling behind, critics will be quick to cry failure when you want to cry success. This is not merely a matter of seeing the glass as half empty or half full, it is an important issue of fact, and as leader it is up to you to make sure that the facts are made clear. If the fact is that the change effort averted or otherwise discouraged a threat, you must make the argument in terms that everyone can understand. If the fact is that the change effort exploited an opportunity in a manner that prevented the organization from falling behind, although it did not advance it much, you must make this argument. In short, a major part of the consolidation of change is making clear what the successes were and how they influence the current and future status of the organization.

Now it is time to celebrate our success, yours and mine. I have nearly finished writing this book, and you have nearly finished reading it. The opportunity to lead an organization toward successful change, change that preserves it and makes it stronger, is both exhilarating and rather daunting. I hope that what you have learned by reading this book proves helpful when that time comes.

Summary

To aid in mastery of this material, summarize it for yourself by filling in this topic outline.

Follow-Through: Institutionalizing Change

I. Four Tasks
  A. Communication
  B. Document updating
  C. Realigning rewards
  D. Culture change

II. What happens next?

III. What is next for you?

IV. A question of politics

V. Celebrate success

Exercises

1. Once again, interview your current or retired organization leader, this time asking questions about institutionalization of change. What role did communications play and how were communications designed to accomplish institutionalization? Were documents updated? If so, what was the process? If not, why not? What role did rewards play in institutionalization? How was culture change assessed? Did it occur? What was done to make sure it occurred? How did the organization mark the end of its change effort? What was done to ensure that future efforts would be less disruptive and expensive? Were change mechanisms maintained, and if so, how? What impact did the change effort and its outcomes have on the leader's career? What advice can he or she give you about dealing with critics and enemies?

2. Ask similar questions of your other interviewees with an eye to how their views differ from those of the leader.

3. Write an essay on institutionalization that outlines your viewpoint and add it to your notebook.

Note

1. Be warned: Much of what is described here borders on or falls within the responsibilities of your human resources unit. It probably has undergone changes along with the rest of the organization and has its own consolidation issues to deal with. Moreover, it probably does not have the extra staff to undertake what is, as you will see, a very considerable job. It is best to include the HR managers in planning the proposed activities and use their help in hiring a consulting firm to do the actual work under their supervision. But, no matter whether it is done in-house, by a consultant, or some combination of the two, the work begins with interviewing you and other relevant persons in order to write the official history.

Sources and Further Reading

Dauten, D. A. (1980). *Quitting: Knowing when to leave.* New York: Walker.

Hambrick, D. C., & Fukutomi, G. D. (1991). The seasons of a CEO's tenure. *Academy of Management Review, 16*, 719–742.

Nadler, D. A. (1998). *Champions of change: How CEOs and their companies are mastering the skills of radical change.* San Francisco: Jossey-Bass.

Seven

Conclusion: Expanding the Analysis of Change Leadership

The preceding chapters were written as though you were the leader of a fairly large commercial organization (although our fictionalized example, Steller Art Frames, was not very big). So to conclude and to deliver on the promise made in the Introduction, let us examine how our analysis of change leadership can be generalized to other kinds of organizations.

Some Differentiations

To begin, we differentiate between leaders who are the executive of their organization (e.g., the CEO or president) and leaders who are the head of a unit of a larger organization (e.g., the vice president for product development or the director of human resources).

Next, we differentiate between for-profit and not-for-profit organizations. For-profit includes most businesses as well as public corporations, such as the Post Office, that are supposed to make money, although they may receive subsidies of some kind. Not-for-profit includes national and international charitable and public service organizations such as the

Your Role	Organization's Purpose	Large Organization	Small Organization
Executive	For profit	Cell #1	Cell #2
Executive	Not for profit	Cell #3	Cell #4
Unit head	For profit	Cell #5	Cell #6
Unit head	Not for profit	Cell #7	Cell #8

Exhibit 7.1   Matrix for Generalizing Our Analysis of Change Leadership to Other Than the Executives of Large Organizations

Muscular Dystrophy Association or CARE, as well as local or regional organizations such as a community food bank or a church. Of course, many local organizations have ties to national and international organizations, but our interest is in those that are largely self-governing.

Finally, we differentiate between large organizations and small organizations; the dividing line is somewhere around 200–300 employees. It is typical of smaller organizations for the owner or the owner's agent to be the executive.

These differentiations yield the matrix in Exhibit 7.1; the numbers in the cells are to identify them in the following discussion.

The Matrix Cells

The previous six chapters have been aimed at leaders of organizations that fall into cell #1. Now we turn to the other cells, some of which are not so different from cell #1, but others of which are different enough to warrant attention.

Cell #2 contains small businesses. You are the CEO, perhaps the owner. The six prime responsibilities apply to you, but you will have fewer people to help you. You may need to hire an assistant to help with assessment of the external environment, culture assessment, and monitoring of implementation progress, but the rest is largely up to you. It will be tempting to simplify the prime responsibilities because they may look too elaborate for a small organization. This probably is an error. Although some simplification is acceptable, if you are serious about change, you must make the change initiative a Big Event so it will be seen as special and important by everyone else. More elaborate measures than you usually would employ, tempered with a bit of good sense, may be just what is needed to signal that you are serious about making change and that you intend to do it well.

The danger is that you may assume you already understand your environment and the culture. Aside from undercapitalization, a major reason for the high failure rate of small businesses is leaders' misunderstanding of their organization's external environment. Until it is too late, they do not recognize threats that their competitors successfully thwart, or they do not recognize opportunities that their competitors successfully exploit. Similarly, leaders often fail to understand the internal environment. Because you are so much a part of your organization, you are deeply enmeshed in its culture. Therefore, you may unable to recognize those aspects of the culture that need changing. Indeed, because things are so familiar to you, you may resist change as much as anyone in the organization. In some ways, leading change in a small business is as difficult as leading it in a large business—different but equally difficult. Leaders of large organizations have to fight organizational inertia. Leaders of small organizations have to fight lack of objective perspective.

Cell #3 contains large not-for-profit organizations. For the most part, your job is much like that of a leader of a large for-profit organization. The main difference is that your organization probably exists to further some issue, from conquering a disease to winning converts to a particular religious or political idea. Your problem is in finding ways to measure the impact you are having and deciding how to increase that impact if it is the kind you want to have. Contributions, increasing membership, and opinion polls are all good, but you may need more if you are trying to make subtle changes. (How can you tell if the research you are supporting actually is making progress toward a cure?) Number of published papers is not necessarily a good measure. Are your converts actually converted, or are they gaining something else by endorsing the cause or idea you are backing? Lip service does not necessarily imply conviction. Similarly, opinion polls are only as good as the questions asked and the sampling techniques used to find respondents, and it takes professionals to do this well. Just any old survey will not do if you are going to use the results to make large changes in your organization.

Cell #4 contains small not-for-profit organizations such as a church or community service organization. Most of what was said for cell #2 applies, as well as what was said for cell #3. What is unique for cell #4 organizations is that their workforce may include a large number of volunteers. Volunteers are difficult to work with because they do not have to put up with being uncomfortable. They can simply walk away. This means that leading change requires considerable interpersonal skills and constant attention to the needs of both the paid employees and the volunteers. It also means that change may take more time because you must avoid stressing volunteers to the point that they depart. If your organization is based on shared ideology, such as a church or a political movement, this task becomes even more difficult. The culture is less flexible when ideology is involved. Changes conflicting with the ideology will meet with even more resistance than changes conflicting with the more mundane parts of the culture. Change is difficult and slow for any organization, but it sometimes is worse for cell #4 organizations.

Cells #5 through #8 represent units within larger organizations. It commonly is said in management courses and business seminars that anyone in an organization can be a leader. This, however, is true only insofar as the person in question has the freedom to undertake the six prime responsibilities described in the previous six chapters. The head of a marketing team may be designated the team leader, but if he or she is given specific instructions about what to accomplish and how to accomplish it, then no matter how much creativity goes into the accomplishment, the designation is merely a title. The person cannot function as a leader in the sense we have been using the term.

On the other hand, heads of units can, in fact, be real leaders. It depends on the degree of autonomy they and their unit have in structuring their affairs in order to meet the threats and opportunities afforded by their external environment. The primary component of a unit's external environment is the larger organization and its vision, goals, plans, and other units' activities. That is, a unit that has sufficient autonomy in fulfilling its obligations to the larger organization offers its head the opportunity to be a true leader.

Cell #5 contains units of large for-profit organizations, units that usually are rather large themselves. Examples would be divisions of a large, diversified automobile company, such as Saturn, which is a division of General Motors, or Kraft Foods, which, at the moment at least, is a division of Altria (which used to be Phillip Morris). The division is, for the most part, a separate business, but its actions are constrained by the parent company's vision, goals, and plans. Within these constraints, the division is given a good deal of freedom in how it conducts business, and it operates as though it belongs in cell #1.

Functional divisions of nondiversified companies also belong to cell #5 if they have sufficient autonomy. For example, the retail banking division of a large bank may have the freedom to create its own vision and plans, albeit constrained by the large bank's vision and plans. It may add new banking products or drop others while implementing its plan, or it may branch out into supermarkets or increase the number of ATMs and determine the price it charges for using them. The head of the division is a leader if he or she pursues a vision that deals with threats, exploits opportunities, and increases the unit's security within the larger structure. The procedures for doing this resemble those for organizations in cell #1, but the external environment includes the politics and constraints of the larger organization as well as the threats and opportunities in the domain of retail banking.

Cell #6 contains units of small businesses, usually with only a few employees (e.g., the product safety group in a small manufacturing company). With the proviso that the unit has a sufficient degree of autonomy, its head may function as a leader by working with the other members of the group as a committee of the whole. The six prime responsibilities are still prime, but their execution is more informal and is overseen by the committee of the whole. Leadership tends to be on a personal level, and the unit members tend to take a more active role in all parts of the process. The unit's external environment includes the politics and constraints of the larger organization as well as the threats and opportunities inherent in its own domain.

Cell #7 contains units of large not-for-profit organizations, such as state chapters of the National Organization of Women (NOW) or local chapters of the Masonic Order. The national organizations are huge, in that they have many chapters and many members. They probably have a national vision (usually based on what they were founded to achieve), but they may do little more than help state or local chapters with their activities rather than dictate what they should do. True, the general spirit of the larger organization sets the direction for the units, but they have considerable autonomy. In this case, the six prime principles strongly apply to the units, and their execution is not very different from the way it would be for an organization in cell # 5 or even cell #1. When there is less autonomy, when the unit is constrained by an articulated national vision and plan, assessment of the unit's external environment must include the politics and constraints of the national organization as well as the more local environment in which it operates.

Cell #8 contains units of small not-for-profit organizations such as a membership drive committee for a community food bank or a docent program for a local museum. These units seldom have much autonomy, but when they do, the six prime responsibilities apply. Given sufficient latitude, the leader of a membership committee can change it to function more profitably within its environment, the larger organization and the outside world of membership solicitation. He or she must understand the culture of the committee (what it is now and what it is striving to become), envision a better future, plan for it, implement that plan, and celebrate success. It's all a matter of proportion and a matter of approaching change in a reasonable way.

A Final Word

I end with a caution. I've presented the material in this book as though leadership of change is largely a cut-and-dried issue: Meet the six prime responsibilities and everything will work out. Of course, this is false. There's nothing cut-and-dried about leadership at any time, least of all during major organizational change. However, to write in less than declarative terms, to include all the conditionals, provisos, and hedging that would properly reflect the way things really are would make every sentence a nightmare of complexity.

Instead, in the interest of clarity, I've relied on your willingness to suspend disbelief long enough to get the essence of each argument. I trust that you'll temper my declarative words with your good sense as you take up your present or future role as a leader. Nothing replaces creativity, ingenuity, intelligence, motivation, and a good sense of humor. No doubt you have all of these, but I hope that what you've learned here will help you use them effectively.

Summary

To aid in the mastery of this material, summarize it for yourself by filling in this topic outline.

Expanding the Analysis of Change

I. Some differentiations
  A. Executive vs. unit head
  B. For-profit vs. not-for-profit
  C. Large vs. small

II. The matrix cells
  A. Cell #1
  B. Cell #2
  C. Cell #3
  D. Cell #4
  E. Cell #5
  F. Cell #6
  G. Cell #7
  H. Cell #8

III. A final word

Exercises

Identify the appropriate matrix cell for the organization in which you have been conducting interviews:

1. If the organization belongs in cell #1, write an essay identifying the major ways in which the change process in the organization differs from what was discussed in Chapters 1 through 6. Speculate on whether those differences are or are not advantageous to the organization and why. Include this essay as the last entry in your notebook.

2. If the organization belongs in a cell other than cell #1, write an essay describing the major ways in which the material in Chapters 1 through 6 must be modified to be used by the organization. Identify the major ways in which the change process in the organization differs from your modified version and speculate on whether these differences are or are not advantageous to the organization and why. Include this essay as the last entry in your notebook.

Appendix A: Assessing Customer Service Needs

The purpose of this appendix is to describe a procedure for identifying areas of potential change in an organization's services in an effort to improve its competitiveness. The Quality Improvement Strategy (QIS, pronounced *kiss*) measures (a) the perceived difference between the services an organization offers and the services customers want (satisfaction) and (b) the perceived difference between the services it offers and the services offered by its competitors (competitiveness). The intersection of dissatisfaction and competitive disadvantage identifies the services that require change (Beach & Burns, 1995; Burns & Beach, 1994).

Logic. The QIS logic rests on the premise that service quality is defined by the customer and involves a comparison of customer expectations with actual service. To measure this, QIS examines the perceived gaps between expectations and services offered by the organization, on one hand, and the perceived gaps between services offered by the organization and services offered by the organization's competitors, on the other hand. This is done by constructing a questionnaire that allows customers to evaluate how the organization now addresses the various services it offers (Now), how it ought to address them (Ought), and how one or more competitors address them (Other).[1]

Measurement. Satisfaction is measured by comparing the average evaluations of Now and Ought to identify the services that customers see the organization as matching (=), exceeding (>), or falling short (<) of their expectations. Note that dissatisfaction is presumed to arise when a service significantly exceeds *or* significantly falls short of customer expectations. Competitiveness is measured by comparing the average evaluations of Now and Other to identify the services that customers see the organization as matching (=), exceeding (>), or falling short (<) of its competitors.

People have difficulty making relative judgments about more than a few services at a time, particularly if those services are very different from each other. Therefore, to make the task easier, the set of services is broken into clusters of conceptually comparable services. Then each respondent, a customer, is asked to (a) prioritize the services in each cluster by ranking them from highest to lowest priority and then to (b) prioritize the clusters by ranking them from highest to lowest priority. These two ranking tasks are done three times for each of the services within a cluster and for each cluster across all clusters, once time each for Now, Other, and Ought.

Computations begin by converting each respondent's ranks within a cluster or across clusters to proportions using the equation:

$$W_i = \frac{N - R_i + 1}{\sum_{i=1}^{N} (N - R_i + 1)},$$

where W_i = a decimal number corresponding to the rank assigned to the *i*th service (*i* = 1 to *N*) or *i*th cluster of services, *N* = the number of services in a cluster or the number of clusters in the questionnaire, and R_i = the rank assigned by the respondent to the *i*th service or *i*th cluster of services. Application of the equation to all ranks within each cluster of services and to all ranks across the clusters of services transforms the ranks into decimal numbers by normalizing them (Stillwell, Seaver, & Edwards, 1981). For example, if there are five services in a cluster (or five clusters of services), the rank of 1 is transformed into .34, the rank of 2 becomes .27, the rank of 3 becomes .20, the rank of 4 becomes .13, and the rank of 5 becomes .06, the sum of which is 1.00. For the aggregated data used in surveys of this kind, the normalization procedure yields a very satisfactory approximation to data obtained from more rigorous measurement methods (Srivastava, Connolly, & Beach, 1995.)

These proportions are inserted into a table like Table A.1, and the indicated computations are performed. The proportion for each service is multiplied by the proportion for the cluster of which it is a member, and the product is multiplied by 100 to produce nondecimal numbers. The

Table A.1   Calculations of Overall Relative Priority ($\times$ 100) for Hypothetical
QIS Data for an Individual Respondent.

Clusters	Relative Cluster Priority	Services	Relative Service Priority	Final Relative Service Priority
Cluster 1	.15	Service 1	.20	.030 × 100 = 3.0*
		Service 2	.15	.022 × 100 = 2.2
		Service 3	.34	.051 × 100 = 5.1
		Service 4	.27	.040 × 100 = 4.0
		Service 5	.06	.009 × 100 = .9
Cluster 2	.20	Service 6	.06	.012 × 100 = 1.2
		Service 7	.27	.054 × 100 = 5.4
		Service 8	.15	.030 × 100 = 3.0
		Service 9	.20	.040 × 100 = 4.0
		Service 10	.34	.068 × 100 = 6.8
Cluster 3	.34	Service 11	.15	.051 × 100 = 5.1
		Service 12	.34	.116 × 100 = 11.6
		Service 13	.20	.068 × 100 = 6.8
		Service 14	.06	.020 × 100 = 2.0
		Service 15	.27	.092 × 100 = 9.2
Cluster 4	.27	Service 16	.20	.054 × 100 = 5.4
		Service 17	.27	.073 × 100 = 7.3
		Service 18	.34	.092 × 100 = 9.2
		Service 19	.15	.040 × 100 = 4.0
		Service 20	.06	.016 × 100 = 1.6
Cluster 5	.06	Service 21	.15	.009 × 100 = .9
		Service 22	.27	.016 × 100 = 1.6
		Service 23	.06	.004 × 100 = .4
		Service 24	.34	.020 × 100 = 2.0
		Service 25	.20	.012 × 100 = 1.2

*i.e., .15 × .20 = .030 × 100 = 3.00

resulting numbers, on the right side of the table, are then averaged across
all respondents for each service. These are the data on which decisions
will be based.

Next, two matched sample t tests are computed across all respondents
for each service, one test for Now versus Other and one test for Now

Table A.2   The QIS Matrix for Identifying Opportunities for Service
Improvement Using Competitiveness (Now minus Other) and
Satisfaction (Now minus Ought).

Competitiveness	Satisfaction		
	Now < Ought	Now = Ought	Now > Ought
Now < Other	Cell #1	Cell #4	Cell #7
Now = Other	Cell #2	Cell #5	Cell #8
Now > Other	Cell #3	Cell #6	Cell #9

versus Ought. Then each service is placed in one of nine cells in the QIS
matrix in Table A.2, depending on the outcomes of the two t tests:
Now < Other, Now = Other, Now > Other cross-classified by Now < Ought,
Now = Ought, and Now > Ought. Assume, for example, that the t test for
customer satisfaction with a given service is significant and negative (i.e.,
Now priority is significantly less than Ought priority) and the t test for
competitiveness also is significant and negative (i.e., Now priority is significantly less than Other priority). The service would belong in cell #1. If
both t tests were insignificant, the service would belong in cell #5; the various combinations of significance for the two tests define where different
services belong.

The QIS matrix. Each cell in the QIS matrix in Table A.2 prescribes a focus
for changing the services that fall in that cell:

Cell #1. Because the organization's priorities are seen by customers as falling
short of its competitors' priorities (Now < Other) for services in this cell, and
because customers are dissatisfied (Now < Ought) with the organization's priorities relative to their expectations, the prescription is to make improvement
of the services a high priority until they match or perceptibly exceed the service
offered by competitors. The goal is to change these services until they move to
cells #4 or #5 but to avoid moving them all the way to cells #7 or #8.

Cell #2. Because the organization matches its competitors' (Now = Other)
priorities for the services in this cell but falls short of customers' expectations
(Now < Ought), competitive advantage can be achieved by giving priority to
changes that make the services perceptibly better than competitors' offerings.
Depending on how easily competitors can improve these services themselves
or how easily outside providers can enter the market, improvements in these
services need not wholly meet customers' expectations; even minimally

perceptible improvements can give the organization a competitive advantage. In general, the goal is to move these services to cell #5 but to avoid moving them all the way to cell #8.

Cell #3. Because the organization exceeds its competitors' (Now > Other) priorities for these services, it already enjoys a competitive advantage, although its offerings fall short of customers' expectations (Now < Ought). Service improvements would strengthen the advantage, but unless improvements are relatively low cost, they might not be worthwhile. If change is worthwhile, the goal is to move the services to cells #5 or #6 but to avoid moving them all the way to cells #8 or #9.

Cells #4, #5, #6. Because customers are satisfied with the organization's (Now = Ought) priorities for the services in these cells, it should make no changes regardless of whether they fall short of (Now < Other), match (Now = Other), or exceed (Now > Other) those of its competitors. Improvements would needlessly divert resources from satisfactory services or from services that need improvement (cells #1, #2, #3).

Cell #7. Although the organization falls short of its competitors' (Now < Other) priorities for services in this cell, customers are dissatisfied (Now > Ought) because the services exceed their expectations. The organization should shift resources from these services to those in cell #1 and allow its competitors to continue to expend their resources on maintaining unnecessarily high quality for these services. The goal is to move these services to cells #4 or #5 but not all the way to cells #1 or #2.

Cell #8. Although the organization matches (Now = Other) its competitors' priorities for these services, it exceeds its customers' expectations (Now > Ought). It should divert resources from these services to those in cell #2, but it also should monitor carefully to see that these services do not decline below the levels offered by competitors. The goal is to move these services to cell #5 but not to cell #2.

Cell #9. The organization exceeds (Now > Other) its competitors' priorities for these services, but it exceeds its customers' expectations (Now > Ought). It should shift resources to the services in cell #3, while monitoring to prevent excessive decline in these services and subsequent customer dissatisfaction. The goal is to move these services to cells #5 or #6 but not to cells #2 or #3.[2]

Decision making. QIS results must not be followed blindly. Clearly, improvement of some services requires more resources than improvement of others. This means that QIS must be regarded as the starting point for a cost-benefit analysis of the services that are identified for change so that prudent use of resources can be achieved. It is quite possible, for example, that improving one or two particularly important and costly services should be linked with improving numerous less important and less costly services. This strategy may result in a far greater overall impact than merely starting at the top of the list and working downward until resources are exhausted. In short, QIS is just the beginning; it forms the foundation for planned change, but it does not provide all the answers. On the other hand, that foundation is considerably more comprehensive than is commonly the case when planning for service improvement is undertaken. The test-retest reliability of results from measurement methods such as the QIS is approximately .70.

An Example

My colleague, Prof. Lawton R. Burns, and I were asked by the planning department of a large hospital (which we will call Central Hospital) to survey local physicians' satisfaction with its services as part of implementing a service improvement program. In the course of discussing the project, it became clear that Central also needed to know how its service offerings were viewed by physicians relative to the offerings of competing hospitals (i.e., competitiveness).

Step 1. We began by identifying the most salient services and service attributes as perceived by physicians. To do this, the planning department compiled a list of 33 of its staff physicians in five medical specialties (medicine, surgery, pediatrics, family practice, and obstetrics/gynecology) who they thought were willing to be interviewed about services that might be sources of satisfaction and dissatisfaction. Some of these physicians were loyal to Central, and others were loyal to Central's competitors. We then conducted half-hour interviews with 15 physicians from the list (3 from each of the five specialties), saving the remainder of the list for a subsequent pilot test. The interviews yielded 25 frequently cited services that could be structured into five clusters of 5 services each.

Step 2. The five clusters of services were used to construct a questionnaire for pilot testing. The questionnaire asked respondents to rank order (from 1 to 5, where 1 = high) both the 5 services in each cluster and the five clusters themselves in three separate exercises to reflect the hospital's allocation of its "attention" to these services. Then these ranks were transformed into decimal numbers using the equation given above and entered in a table like Table A.1. In the first exercise, physicians ranked in terms of the relative amount of attention that Central *now* allocates to each of the 5 services in each cluster or each of the five clusters themselves. In the second exercise, physicians ranked in terms of the relative amount of attention that some *other* competing hospital presently allocates. In the third exercise, physicians ranked in terms of the relative amount of attention that Central *ought* to allocate to the services or clusters of services.[3]

Attention was used rather than *priority, satisfaction,* or *importance* because it is fairly neutral; *priority* has a particularly urgent and value-laden connotation. Our aim was to learn what physicians perceived Central (Now) and its competitors (Other) to be doing uncolored, as much as possible, by value judgments. Such judgments were reserved for the Ought rankings. The comparisons dictated by the cells of Table A.2 were to be the substance of the quantitative results reported to Central.

Step 3. The questionnaires were sent to 1,260 local physicians in the five specialties. After some prompting, 768 (61%) of the questionnaires were returned, of which 586 (76%) were filled out correctly.

Step 4. For each physician, we applied the transformation equation to the ranks assigned by him or her to each of the 5 services within each cluster and to the five clusters themselves. This yielded five decimal weights (that summed to 1.00) in each cluster and one set of five weights (that summed to 1.00) for the five clusters themselves. The multiplications illustrated in Table A.1 were then performed using these numbers ($\times$ 100), and the means and standard deviations for each service and for each cluster of services were calculated across physicians. This permitted computations of matched-sample *t* tests for differences between Central Now and Other (competitiveness) and between Central Now and Central Ought (satisfaction).

Results. Comparison of Central Now and Central Ought revealed numerous differences between how Central Hospital presently allocates its attention across services and how physicians think that its attention ought to be allocated (Satisfaction). Statistically significant differences ($p < .05$, although the particular significance level used is rather arbitrary; because one is running multiple *t* tests, it should be relatively conservative) identified services in which Central either exceeds or falls short of the physicians' expectations; insignificant differences identified services in which Central meets physicians' expectations.

Comparison of Central Now and Other hospitals showed there are substantial differences between how Central and its competitors presently allocate their attention to the 25 services (competitiveness). Statistically significant differences ($p < .05$) identified services in which Central either exceeds or falls short of its competition; insignificant differences identified services in which Central matches its competitors.

The managerial implications of these significant and insignificant differences became clear when the 25 services were sorted into the cells in a QIS matrix like the one in Table A.2. Nothing would be gained by presenting the detailed results here. Suffice it that the services were spread throughout the cells, with particular concentrations in cells #1, #2, #8, and #9 (further analyses of the various physician specialties broke these results out in greater detail, especially when there were bimodal distributions of differences). That is, the results were concentrated in cells defined by low satisfaction due to failing to meet physician's expectations coupled with falling short of or merely matching the competition's offerings or by low satisfaction due to exceeding physician's expectations coupled with matching or exceeding the competition's offerings.

Decision making. Of course, prescriptions for service improvement had to be tempered by the availability of money and other resources. They also had to be driven by the reasons physicians gave for the evaluations.

After the services had been sorted into a table like Table A.2, focus groups composed of physicians from each of the specialty areas were convened to obtain qualitative information about what the results meant in terms of concrete steps that could be taken to improve services. These groups discussed the reasons why physicians prioritized the various services the way they did and suggested changes that would improve service. By concentrating on the QIS results, the discussions tended to be very practical and very informative. The suggestions provided Central's leaders with specific targets for change, particularly the services in cells #1, #2, #8, and #9.

Notes

1. Appendix B contains a questionnaire of the general form being proposed, although it uses only one evaluation instead of three and requires the distribution of points rather than ranking.

2.   Cells #2, #4, #5, #6, and #8 all represent services for which Now is not statistically different from Other or Ought. The absence, however, of a statistically significant difference may not indicate equality. One should look closely at the distribution of differences (Now minus Other or Now minus Ought across customers for a given service). Different distributions have different implications. A distribution that is unimodal at zero indicates that the customers do not all agree about the direction or magnitude of the difference, but the general consensus is that it tends toward zero. It is best to plot the data as a cumulative frequency distribution across differences, in which case a unimodal distribution is revealed as an S-shaped curve. A distribution of differences that is uniform indicates that there is no consensus among the customers about the difference. The cumulative plot of a uniform distribution is a straight line. A distribution of differences that is multimodal indicates that there are subgroups of customers who hold different opinions about the difference. The cumulative plot of a multimodal distribution produces a function that, although always increasing, has changes of slope in it corresponding to the various modes. When a multimodal distribution is found for a service, it may prove valuable to break out the subgroups of customers corresponding to the various modes in order to better understand the results.

3.   These tasks were counterbalanced across respondents to control for order effects.

Sources and Further Reading

Beach, L. R., & Burns, L. R. (1995). The service quality improvement strategy: Identifying priorities for change. *International Journal of Service Industry Management, 5,* 5–15.

Burns, L. R., & Beach, L. R. (1994). The quality improvement strategy. *Health Care Management Review, 19,* 21–31.

Srivastava, J., Connolly, T., & Beach, L. R. (1995). Do ranks suffice? A comparison of alternative weighting approaches in value elicitation. *Organizational Behavior and Human Decision Processes, 63,* 112–116.

Stillwell, W. G., Seaver, D. A., & Edwards, W. (1981). A comparison of weight approximation techniques in multiattribute decision making. *Organization Behavior and Human Performance, 28,* 62–77.

Appendix B: The Organizational Culture Survey

The following is a questionnaire that has been used extensively to assess organizational culture (Weatherly, 1995; Weatherly & Beach, 1996). The specific constituents in the questionnaire have wide applicability, but it is prudent to revise them to fit the particular organization you want to assess. To do this, interview people throughout the organization, asking them to describe the organization and what it values. Condense the lists to the most frequently mentioned values and revise the questionnaire accordingly. Remember to keep the values in any cluster fairly comparable and keep the number of values in the clusters roughly equal, or respondents will have difficulty making their judgments.

Instructions

An organization's culture is its personality. And like the personality of an individual person, it can be described by the relative salience of its various characteristics, beliefs, and values. Thus one might say of a friend that he or she is very friendly, somewhat sensitive, a bit aggressive. So too one can say of an organization that it strongly possesses characteristic X, has little of characteristic Y, exhibits nothing of characteristic Z.

The purpose of this survey is to permit you to describe the personality (the culture) of the organization for which you work. This will be done by evaluating three major parts of your organization's culture: the part that relates to employee welfare, the part that relates to doing the job, and the part that relates to the goals of the organization.

Evaluation will be done, first, by considering each of these three parts of the culture separately and dividing up points among their constituents in order to indicate the relative salience of each in your organization's culture *as it is, not as you might wish it to be.*

To fill out the survey, turn to the next page and read each of the five short paragraphs about the part of the culture as it relates to the employees. Then divide 100 points among the five paragraphs to indicate the relative degree (percentage) to which the topic of each is salient in your organization's culture (a greater percentage of the 100 points means more salience). Please sum your percentages to make sure they add up to 100 percent. Then follow the same procedure for the part of the culture that relates to doing the job and for the part of the culture that relates to the organization's goals.

Finally, on the last page, please divide 100 points among the three parts of your organization's culture (employees, job, and organizational goals) to indicate their relative salience in the overall culture.

The Organizational Culture Survey

PART I: The Culture As It Relates to How Employees Should Be Treated and the Opportunities Afforded Them

_____ **Respect:** Recognizes that employees are important, that they have a need to maintain their self respect and dignity, and that they have a right to a voice in matters that concern them.

_____ **Growth:** Encourages career development and personal growth through improvement of skills and knowledge.

_____ **Rewards:** Rewards excellence with recognition, increased income, promotion, and privileges.

_____ **Communication:** Promotes openness and the free flow of information among levels of the organization and between and within departments.

_____ **Fairness:** Emphasizes equitable treatment of all employees.

_____ **Total Points (Should = 100%)**

PART II: The Culture As It Relates to Professionalism and to Organizational Support of Efforts to Do a Good job

_____ **Effectiveness:** Defines job success as contributing to the accomplishment of the organization's general goals as well as to the accomplishment of specific departmental goals.

_____ **Efficiency:** Emphasizes doing things correctly and well and adapting new or alternative ways of doing things if they contribute to efficiency.

_____ **Support:** Provides the necessary resources for doing the job well.

_____ **Innovation:** Fosters creative problem solving at all levels of the organization and supports reasonable risk taking.

_____ **Enjoyment:** Recognizes that obtaining pleasure from one's job is itself desirable and that doing so contributes to the climate and stability of the organization

_____ **Total Points (Should = 100%)**

PART III: The Culture As It Relates to How the Organization Interfaces With Its Environment and Strives to Accomplish Its Mission

_____ **Achievement:** Strives to accomplish the organization's mission and to attain its goals.

_____ **Competitiveness:** Seeks to increase the organization's standing relative to its competitors in terms both of its profitability and of its ability to serve its customers and expand its market share.

_____ **Resourcefulness:** Attempts to create new concepts and recognize new opportunities, and to move quickly to take advantage of both of them.

_____ **Judgment:** Tries to identify and effectively deal with the rapidly changing hazards in the business environment as well as the challenges presented by competitors' special strengths.

_____ **Integrity:** Adheres to both stated and unstated moral and ethical codes and pursues quality, honor, and trustworthiness in all business transactions and personal dealings.

_____ **Total Points (Should = 100%)**

PART IV: All Three Parts Together

The Organization's Overall Culture:

_____ As related to employee treatment and opportunities: Respect, Growth, Rewards, Communications, Fairness

_____ As related to professionalism and support: Effectiveness, Efficiency, Support, Innovation, Enjoyment

_____ As related to how the organization interfaces with its environment and accomplishes its mission: Achievement, Competitiveness, Resourcefulness, Judgment, Integrity

_____ **Total Points (Should = 100%)**

Computations

To derive an individual respondent's view of the relative salience or priority of the 15 values in the organization's culture, begin by converting all of the points in the respondent's survey to decimal numbers (for example, 5 points becomes .05). Next, construct a score sheet similar to Table A.1 in Appendix A. To do this, substitute Parts I, II, and III of the Organizational Culture Survey for the five clusters in the left column. Then enter the corresponding numbers from Part IV of the survey in the column directly to the right of each of the three parts to indicate the relative priority of each of the three parts.

Next, replace the Service 1, Service 2, and so forth, in the Services column with the labels of each of the 5 values in Parts I, II, and III, respectively, and enter their corresponding decimal numbers from the respondent's survey to indicate the relative priority of each value.

Next, multiply the relative priority number for each part (second column) and the relative priority number for each value (fourth column) for every one of the 5 values in each part, and multiply each of these answers by 100 (merely to get rid of the decimal points). Enter each of these last numbers in the column on the far right of the score sheet to indicate the final relative priority to the respondent of each of the 15 characteristics in the survey. (If you did the arithmetic correctly, the sum of the numbers in this column will be very close to 100).

For multiple respondents, means of the final relative priorities (the column of numbers on the right of each respondent's score sheet) can be calculated across respondents for each of the 15 values to yield a more stable measure of the organization's culture, the relative mean priority (or salience) of each value. The variance associated with these means indicates the degree of disagreement among the respondents.

Presentation of results

The mean relative salience of each of the 15 values is best summarized as a profile. Bar graphs are technically more appropriate, but profiles are customarily used in personality assessment and therefore are used for these results. See Appendix C for further discussion of this technique and an example of a profile for an organization's culture (Figure C.5). See Appendix A for an example using ranks instead of points.

Sources and Further Reading

Weatherly, K. A. (1995). *The rapid assessment of organizational culture using the Organizational Culture Survey: Theory, research and application.* Unpublished doctoral dissertation, University of Arizona, Tucson.

Weatherly, K. A., & Beach, L. R. (1996). Organizational culture and decision making. In L. R. Beach (Ed.), *Decision making in the workplace: A unified perspective.* Mahwah, NJ: Erlbaum.

Appendix C:
Decision Techniques

I f you are like most decision makers faced with a murky situation, your first impulse is to get more information. Unfortunately, if the situation is murky, it usually isn't clear what information you need. A great deal of time and money can be wasted in obtaining facts and figures that, in the end, prove irrelevant. The good news is that you often know more than you realize, but the knowledge is so unstructured that it is of little use. Therefore, the first step in clarifying a murky decision is to draw a coherent picture of what you know about it.

- The very act of creating a coherent picture of the decision tends to add to your understanding of it.
- A coherent picture provides structure for what you already know.
- A coherent picture indicates what you do not know, thus guiding your search for relevant information.
- A coherent picture often makes the right decision so obvious that you need not waste time on further deliberation.

There are many techniques for creating pictures of decisions. Because of space limitations, the following discussion will concentrate on four kinds that are particularly cogent to the decisions that have been discussed throughout this book. The first kind—influence diagrams, matrices, and trees—clarifies forecasts; they indicate what leads to what and what causes what. The second kind, value trees, clarifies understanding about the standards that are applicable to the decision. The third kind, compatibility matrices, aids in the appraisal of options' compatibility with applicable standards in order to screen out those options that are not of sufficient quality to be acceptable. The fourth kind, decision matrices and decision trees, aids in the appraisal of the potential yield of options in order to choose the best option.

Influence Diagrams, Matrices, and Trees

Forecasting

The human mind is a forecasting device. We formulate rules about what leads to what in order to forecast (predict) future events. The primary rules predict what to expect in the normal course of things: if A, then B. Secondary rules predict how things will be affected by our own or other people's actions: if A, and one does C, then D will occur instead of B. In the former case, we see event B as being caused by event A. In the latter case, we see event D as being caused by our own action, C, in the context of A. The first rule forecasts what would happen if we did not intervene, and the second rule forecasts what will happen if we do intervene. Both rules are about what to expect and about to what to attribute the occurrence of the final event.

Most people possess numerous forecasting rules that are not particularly accurate (racial, sexual, and other kinds of stereotypes are faulty forecasting rules). One often hears people insist that if an event occurs, another event will happen. If you cite a case in which such an event occurred and the predicted event did *not* happen, you are told that it is the exception that proves the rule. It is difficult to argue against a strongly held rule.

Influence Analysis

The purpose of influence analysis is to see if a forecasting rule that you suspect to be reliable really is. Let us begin with the special case of forecasts based on a single influence. Figure C.1 shows three kinds of pictures of influence (causality), followed by a step-by-step procedure for doing an influence analysis.

Diagram. At the top of Figure C.1, we simply diagram the cause (A) and the effect (B) and connect them with an arrow to indicate the direction of causality. This is not very difficult, but it is not very valuable either.

Matrix. A more enlightening way of picturing causality is in terms of the degree to which it is either *deterministic* or *probabilistic* (i.e., the degree to

Diagram

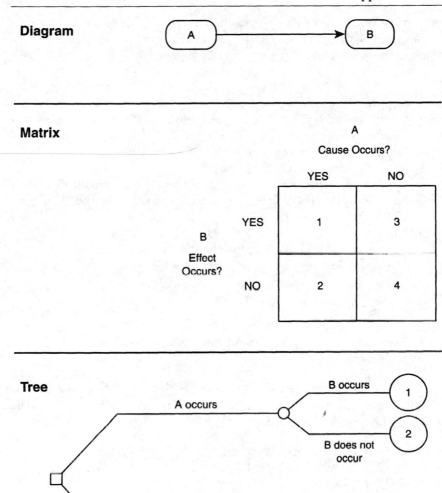

Matrix

Tree

Figure C.1   Three Kinds of Pictures of Influence (Causality)

which the cause reliably produces the effect). In a strict sense, the word *cause* means deterministic, just as *influence* means probabilistic, but we will use the words interchangeably. The steps in producing an influence matrix are:

- Step 1. Identify the cause (A) and the effect (B).
- Step 2a. Define the effect (B) clearly in terms that allow an observer to know when it occurs and when it does not occur.
- Step 2b. Do the same for the cause (A).
- Step 3. Construct an "influence matrix."
- Step 4. Gather information about each cell in the matrix in an effort to see how reliably the effect occurs when the cause occurs or does not occur when that cause does not occur.
- Step 5. If information does not exist for one or more cells,
  - conclude that causality is neither established nor refuted, or
  - do an experiment that will produce the needed information.

- Step 6. Assess causality:
  - Deterministic causality
  - Probabilistic causality.

- Step 7. Draw conclusions about the original question in light of your assessment.

The influence matrix helps in the assessment of the strength of the relationship between events A and B. It requires that one think about the reliability of the contingencies in each matrix cell:

- Cell 1. If A occurs, does B occur?
- Cell 2. If A occurs, does B fail to occur?
- Cell 3. If A does not occur, does B occur anyway?
- Cell 4. If A does not occur, does B fail to occur?

One way of getting data for the matrix is merely to recall instances that fall in each cell. This requires great care because it is prone to subjective biases and may not produce satisfactory results. Moreover, what might convince one person may not convince another, so one's recollections are unlikely to be of much value in organizational decision making. It is far better to use the memories of as many people as possible, and hard data are even better.

The matrix cells reveal exactly what data to gather. Rather than merely gathering confirmatory data (cells 1 and 4), you need to know if there are disconfirmatory data (cells 2 and 3). Hard data can be obtained by looking back through records or by actually doing some sort of experiment in which it is possible to see how frequently events in each of the cells are observed.

An example: It is widely believed that productivity is influenced by employees' job satisfaction. The forecast is that if job satisfaction can be increased, productivity will increase. This forecasting rule, however, is not sufficiently robust to be of much use. True, there is a tendency for satisfied people to be more productive, but the data from countless scientific studies show that the tendency is very slight (the average correlation is about .17). Although this unexpectedly poor result is found time and again, people are so convinced that the forecasting rule is right that they refuse to believe the data. A great deal of effort has gone into attempts to increase job satisfaction in the hope of increasing productivity, and it was wasted. (In case you are wondering why the rule is wrong, it may be because even workers who are very dissatisfied have to produce at least enough to keep their jobs, so below some level of satisfaction, productivity does not go down any further. Trying to make these dissatisfied workers more satisfied will not pay off in increased productivity until they have been moved above that critical level.)

Tree. The lower part of Figure C.1 translates the influence matrix into an influence tree. Both the matrix and the tree contain the same information, but some people find the tree provides a clearer picture. Starting at the left of the tree, the cause (A) either occurs or does not, whereupon the effect (B) either occurs or does not. The numbers at the ends of the branches of the tree indicate the corresponding cells in the matrix. If observations— say, in the form of frequencies—have been entered in the cells, they can be written on the sloping lines leading from the cause (A occurs or does not occur) to the effect (B occurs or does not occur).

Of course, not all causal rules involve only one cause. Figure C.2 contains illustrations of an influence diagram and an influence tree for two causes. Note that there is no matrix because it would have to be in three dimensions; a causal rule with three causes would require a four-dimensional matrix, and so forth. By being creative, it is possible to draw three- and four-dimensional matrices, but they are more confusing than no matrix at all and probably should be avoided. Indeed, although influence trees can be expanded to include many causes, they quickly become unwieldy. For very complicated causal rules, it is best to stay with influence diagrams. For example, Figure C.3 contains a more complex example

Diagram

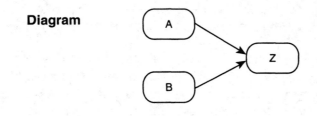

Tree

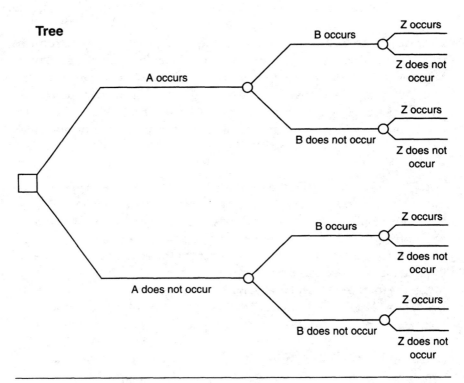

Figure C.2   Influence Diagram and Tree for Multiple Causes

of a diagram for a town that is considering the purchase of a landfill site (garbage dump). The town wants to stop using the county's site because the fees are high, but if it uses a site within the town limits, the people who live in the area are bound to be unhappy. The diagram is an attempt to describe the dilemma.

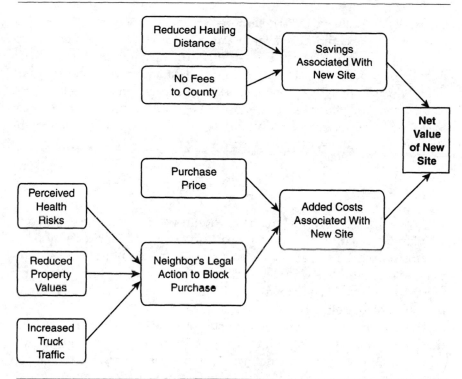

Figure C.3   Influence Diagram for a Town's Decision About Opening Its Own Landfill Site

There are numerous books that explain how to construct and use both simple and complex influence diagrams, and the interested reader is referred to them. A simple, easily understood introduction is contained in Robert Clemen's *Making Hard Decisions* (1991).

Influence diagrams, matrices, and trees become valuable during vision building and during planning. Although it may not be stated as such, an action that is proposed as a way of achieving a goal is, in fact, being proposed as a cause that will produce the desired effect, goal achievement. The forecast is that if in situation A, you do C, the result will be D. Situation A is either the present circumstances or some set of circumstances that will occur in the future. Action C is the action that is being proposed to achieve a desirable goal, D. The decision facing the vision-building group or the planning committee is whether to adopt action C as an element of the vision or the plan. The dilemma is that it is not clear that

C actually will achieve D. To determine whether it will or not, data can be gathered from examining similar instances in the experience of the group members (dangerous because it depends on their recollections, which may be biased) or by gathering objective data about the experiences of other organizations. The pronouncements of experts, business school professors, and consultants on the topic may be regarded as data too, because these people supposedly have attempted to gather objective data to substantiate the reliability of various forecasting rules.

Value Trees

In day-to-day decision making, it is seldom necessary to make decision standards explicit, though they are part of the decision maker's thinking when the decision is made. However, because vision building and planning already require one to step back and think about the big picture, it is worthwhile to take time to make the decision standards as clear as possible. The tool for doing this is called a *value tree*.

The influence trees in Figures C.1 and C.2 grew from left to right. Value trees grow from top to bottom, as in Figure C.4. Note that the highest level (supra level) is very broadly defined. Perhaps it is the organization's culture, its vision, or its current plan. Perhaps it is something more limited, like "our current human resources program." Whatever it is, it is the *topic* that will be analyzed into *elements* that that then will be given *weights* to indicate their relative importance as decision standards. Figure C.4 contains step-by-step instructions about how to construct value trees and there are examples of their use in Appendixes A and B.

Decomposition

The reasoning behind the hierarchical construction of value trees is that it is difficult for people to keep all of the relevant elements of a decision in mind at any one time. Thus, construction of the tree begins with the topic (supra level), decomposes it into major clusters (level 2), and decomposes these clusters into fairly concrete elements (level 3) that often are unique to the particular topic under consideration. Then decision makers must subjectively assign relative weights to the clusters (level 2) to indicate their importance (or salience, contribution, priority, or whatever is cogent) to the decision topic. One way of doing this is to rank the clusters

Step 1   Name the supra level topic.
Step 2   Decompose to levels 2 and 3 (or more if appropriate).
Step 3   Construct the value tree.

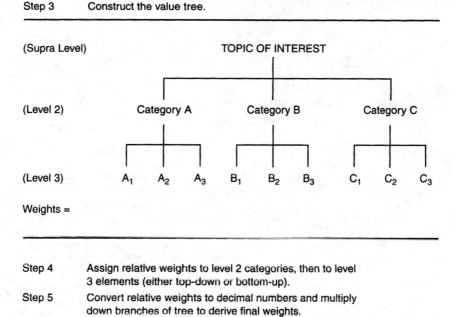

(Supra Level)   TOPIC OF INTEREST

(Level 2)   Category A   Category B   Category C

(Level 3) A_1 A_2 A_3 B_1 B_2 B_3 C_1 C_2 C_3

Weights =

Step 4   Assign relative weights to level 2 categories, then to level
           3 elements (either top-down or bottom-up).
Step 5   Convert relative weights to decimal numbers and multiply
           down branches of tree to derive final weights.

Figure C.4   Steps in Constructing a Value Tree

(Appendix A) and another is to divide up 100 points among the clusters according to their relative importance (Appendix B). We will use the points method in what follows.

Within each cluster individually, the decision maker must indicate the relative weights of the elements (level 3). This is done separately for each cluster on level 2. Finally, the weights on each level are turned into proportions. (The weights for level 2 sum to 1.00; the weights for the elements in each of the parts sum to 1.00). Then one multiplies the weights down the branches of the tree to derive relative weights at the tips of each branch; these weights sum to 1.00 across all of the elements on level 3. These final weights, usually multiplied by 100 to get rid of decimals (called "normalizing"), indicate the *relative* importance of each of the elements of the supra level topic.

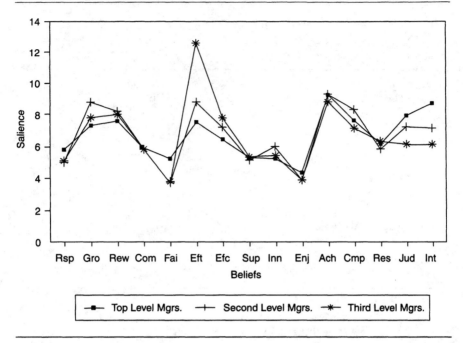

Figure C.5   Culture Profiles for the Managers, Supervisors, and Employees of
a State Agency

The Results

To display the results of the value tree, plot a graph of the final weights
of the elements (bottom of a tree) to obtain a profile of the relative importance of the elements. The profile of an organization's culture in Figure C.5
is an example of such a graph. The points on the graph are the averages of
the normalized weights obtained from the managers, supervisors, and
frontline employees of a comptroller's office who filled out the questionnaire in Appendix B. Kept handy during decision deliberation, profiles
such as these help you keep in mind what is valuable to the organizations
and what is not, thus helping you design a vision or plan that is compatible with those values.

If value trees seem a little complicated, it is because they are harder to
describe than to construct.

Step 1   Construct and use a Value Tree (Figure C.4) to ascertain relative weights of relevant values (Standards).

Step 2   Construct a Compatability Matrix with values and their relative weights along the top and decision options down the side.

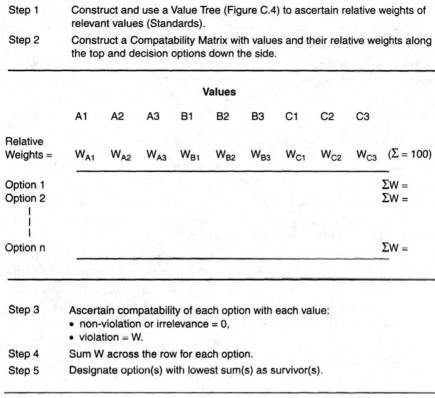

Values

	A1	A2	A3	B1	B2	B3	C1	C2	C3	
Relative Weights =	W_{A1}	W_{A2}	W_{A3}	W_{B1}	W_{B2}	W_{B3}	W_{C1}	W_{C2}	W_{C3}	$(\Sigma = 100)$
Option 1										$\Sigma W =$
Option 2										$\Sigma W =$
Option n										$\Sigma W =$

Step 3   Ascertain compatability of each option with each value:
   • non-violation or irrelevance = 0,
   • violation = W.

Step 4   Sum W across the row for each option.

Step 5   Designate option(s) with lowest sum(s) as survivor(s).

Figure C.6   Steps in Performing a Compatibility Test Using a Compatibility Matrix

Compatibility Matrices

Value trees provide a picture of the relative importance of the standards that govern a decision. It often is necessary, however, to go a step further in order to assess the compatibility of options with these standards in order to discard those that are incompatible.

Figure C.6 contains step-by-step instructions about how to perform a compatibility test for option adoption after the relevant standards have been obtained using a value tree. The basic idea is quite simple. The values' (standards') names and their relative importance weights from the tips of the value tree's branches are arrayed across the top of the compatibility matrix. The options (ideas for goals or plans) are listed down the left side of the matrix. Then each option is considered in relation to each value. If the option is judged to be compatible with the value or irrelevant to it, a zero is written in the matrix cell. If the option violates the value—that is, if it negates, contravenes, prevents, retards, or in any significant way interferes with or contradicts the value—the value's relative weight (at the top of the column) is written in the cell. After all values have been considered for an option, the weights in the cells are summed across the row, and the sum is written at the end of the row. This is done for each of the options separately. The sums indicate the degree of compatibility of each option with the values. The lower the sum, the greater the compatibility. The larger the sum, the greater the reason to reject the option's inclusion in the vision or plan.

After the sums of weights are written on the right of the matrix for all options, it is time to select the ones that are to be survivors. By this time, most decision makers have a fairly clear idea of which should survive; they can spot the losers even if they cannot identify the best of the winners. Rejecting losers permits attention to be focused on the winners, either to gather more information or simply choose the best from among them.

Midlevel options (neither very high sums, nor very low) often present a problem because there is doubt about whether they are winners or losers. Given this doubt, it is better to let an option survive than to reject it, but only if there are other survivors. The reason for this is that the doubtful option can receive a more thorough evaluation during the choice process. If the doubtful option is the only one being considered, however, or if it would be the only survivor out of a number of options, it should *not* be allowed to survive. This is because a single survivor tends to be adopted as the default, and if one is not even sure this option ought to survive to be in the choice set, one certainly cannot be sure that it ought to be the final choice.

Decision Matrices, Equations, and Trees

Decision matrices, equations, and trees are the most frequently prescribed methods for making choices of the best option from among the survivors of the quality test. Figure C.7 contains a matrix, its equivalent mathematical equations, and its equivalent decision tree, followed by the steps in the construction of a decision tree. Each is a picture of the choice, but the matrix is less flexible than the tree, and the tree is less flexible than the equations.

That is, it is difficult to represent choices among very many alternative options in matrix form, and trees get very "bushy." Similarly, if the options have many potential outcomes, matrices and trees get very complicated. Equations get complicated too, but the rules of algebra serve to keep the complexity under control.

Utility

Because choice looks at the relative quantity of options' potential yields rather than at merely whether each option is or is not sufficiently compatible with standards, decision matrices and trees must permit comparisons among options. The potential yield of an option is commonly referred to as its utility. *Utility* is a psychological concept. It indicates the private worth to a decision maker of the outcomes that selection of a particular option (usually a course of action) may eventually yield. Often it is assumed that the utility for money is exactly the same as the amount of money (linear with money), but in reality, the richer one is, the less an additional unit of money is worth (called decreasing marginal utility for money). For convenience, however, we will regard utility and money as much the same.

Even money is not constant in value. If I know that I definitely will receive $X, that amount of money is worth more to me than if I only have a chance of receiving it. That is, any doubt about receiving $X in the future acts to discount its value to me at this moment. For example, I am less willing to work hard now if I only *think* I will be paid $X tomorrow than if I *know* I will be paid $X tomorrow. This is customarily represented in decision analyses by multiplying the amount in question, $X, by the probability of receiving it, P. Because P is a decimal number between .00 and 1.00, it reduces $X in proportion to my doubt. Thus, if the probability of getting paid $5 tomorrow is .90, I will work harder than if the probability is only .40 because $5 multiplied by .90 = $4.50, versus $5 multiplied by .40 = $2.00. This product is called an *expected value*.

Matrix

Consider the matrix in Figure C.7. Let us suppose that the decision involves choosing either A or B, both of which have met the standards necessary to survive the compatibility analysis. Suppose further that either choice can lead to only two possible states, 1 or 2, and the probabilities are .80 and .20 for each. The entries in the cells of the matrix describe the outcomes, the payoffs, that will result from choosing one or the other option and having one or the other state subsequently occur. Thus, if you choose option A and state 1 occurs, you will gain $5. If you choose option A and state 2 occurs, you lose $7. If you choose option B, the results are similar except the payoffs are different. The question is which option should you choose?

Equations

The decision strategy described by Figure C.7 dictates that to choose the best option, you should calculate the total expected value for each option and select the option for which this total is largest. This is called *maximizing expected value,* and it is represented for the matrix by the two equations in Figure C.7. In words, the first equation says that the expected value for option A is equal to the probability of state 1 occurring if you were to select A times the payoff of $5, plus the probability of state 2 occurring if you select A times the loss of $7. This results in a total expected value for option A of $2.60, which is a gain. Following the same procedure for option B produces a negative total expected value of –$3.60, which is a loss. Maximization, and common sense, requires you to choose option A because it has the best expected value. (There is not always a gain and a loss. Sometimes there are two gains, and you then choose the option with the larger of the two. Or there may be two losses, and you then choose the option with the smaller of the two.)

Tree

The decision tree in Figure C.7 is equivalent to the matrix and the equations. The little box on the left stands for a choice (between A or B). The circles at the forks stand for the occurrence of an event, either state 1 or state 2. The probabilities are written on the slanted lines at the forks, and the payoffs are written at the ends of the branches. The expected values for each of the options are written in bubbles with arrows aimed at the event forks. Option A *dominates* option B because A has a greater expected value—that is, the quantity of A's potential yield is greater than B's, and consequently A is the best choice. The steps in constructing a decision tree are:

Matrix

States

1 (0.8)   2 (0.2)

	1	2
A	$5	-$7
B	-$6	$6

Options

Equations

$EV_A = P\ U_{A1} + (1 - P)\ U_{A2} = 0.8\ (\$5) + 0.2\ (-\$7) = \$2.6$

$EV_B = P\ U_{B1} + (1 - P)\ U_{B2} = 0.8\ (-\$6) + 0.2\ (-\$6) = -\$3.6$

Tree

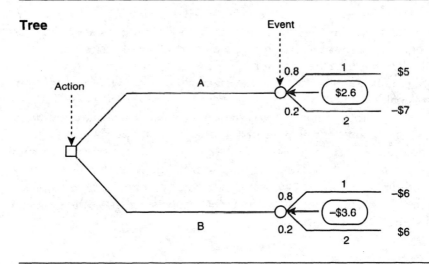

Figure C.7   Three Pictures of Choice

- Step1. Identify decision to be addressed. Define in terms of the problem, not solutions.
- Step 2. Identify alternative solutions.
- Step 3. Identify choices and events:
  - Choices are under your control.
  - Events are partly or wholly externally controlled.

- Step 4. Construct the tree:
  - Choices first
  - Events next

- Step 5. Assign payoffs to the tips of the branches.
- Step 6. Assign probabilities to event nodes.
- Step 7. Ascertain expected values of the choice nodes.
- Step 8. Determine the dominant choice.

The techniques described here are only a few that scientists have devised to help decision makers construct pictures of their decisions, thereby helping them better understand those decisions. As doubtless you realize, none of these techniques can be used in a blind, mechanical manner: They require a degree of creative thought. So too, simple as they are, they still are too cumbersome for use on very simple decision problems. Their value lies in use on decisions for which you need a little help in clarifying the issues and keeping track of the broader implications. For this reason, they are especially appropriate for strategic decisions about the goals that are to be adopted for the organization's vision and the plans that are to be adopted to guide the organization's activities in achieving those goals.

In spite of their complexity, these techniques are considerably simpler and easier to use than they at first appear. Extreme precision seldom is needed, and the picture you draw of the decision often can be a fairly rough approximation. After all, the purpose of drawing the picture is to clarify your thinking, not to automate the decision by removing you from the process. Used with care, and with a bit of skepticism, these techniques can be helpful.

Sources and Further Reading

Beach, L. R., & Connolly, T. (2005). *The psychology of decision making* (2nd ed.). Thousand Oaks, CA: Sage.

Clemen, R. T. (1991). *Making hard decisions.* Boston: PWS—Kent.

About the Author

Lee Roy Beach is McClelland Professor Emeritus of Management and Policy at the Eller College of Management, University of Arizona, Tucson. He received his PhD in Psychology from the University of Colorado and began his professional career in human factors research for the U.S. Navy, followed by service at the Office of Naval Research in Washington, D.C. After leaving the Navy, he completed 2 years of postdoctoral work in the psychology of decision making at the University of Michigan. He then joined the Cognitive and the Organizational Psychology programs at the University of Washington, where he moved from assistant to full professor, served as Chair of the Psychology Department, received the Alumni Award for Distinguished Teaching, was named Professor of the Year for the State of Washington and Bronze Medallist for National Professor of the Year for 1989, received the Feldman Award for research, and was named to the University Teaching Academy. He has been a Visiting Scholar at Cambridge and Leiden Universities and a Visiting Professor of Business at the University of Chicago. After joining the management college at Arizona, he was named Professor of the Year for 1998, served for 3 years as Vice Dean, taught graduate and executive education courses, and continued his research and consulting. He is a Fellow of both the American Psychological Association and the American Psychological Society and a charter member of the latter. He is the author of over 125 scholarly articles and six books on organizational behavior and decision making, the latest of which is *The Psychology of Decision Making* (2nd ed., 2005), coauthored with his colleague Terry Connolly and published by Sage.

Index

CPSIA information can be obtained
at www.ICGtesting.com
Printed in the USA
FSOW01n1352170917
38768FS